The Gospel of Mark

OneBook.

DAILY–WEEKLY

The Gospel of Mark

Brad Johnson

 Seedbed

Scripture quotations, unless otherwise marked, are taken from the Revised Standard Version of the Bible, copyright 1952 [2nd edition, 1971] by the Division of Christian Education of the National Council of the Churches of Christ in the United States of America. Used by permission. All rights reserved.

Scripture quotations marked GNT (Greek New Testament) are from the Novum Testamentum Graece, Nestle-Aland 27h Edition. Copyright (c) 1993 Deutsch Bibelgesellschaft, Stuttgart. Used by permission.

The Works of Josephus: Complete and Unabridged in One Volume (New Updated Edition), trans. by William Whiston, A.M. (Peabody, MA: Hendrickson Publishers, 1987).

Printed in the United States of America
Library of Congress Control Number: 2016958434

Cover design by Strange Last Name
Page design and layout by PerfecType

Johnson, Bradley T., 1965-
   The Gospel of Mark / Brad Johnson. – Frankin, Tennessee : Seedbed Publishing, ©2017.

   x, 166 pages ; 21 cm. + 1 videodisc – (OneBook. Daily-weekly)

   ISBN 9781628243741 (pbk. : alk. paper)
   ISBN 9781628243789 (DVD)
   ISBN 9781628243758 (mobipocket ebk.)
   ISBN 9781628243765 (epub ebk.)
   ISBN 9781628248772 (updf ebk.)

   1. Bible. Mark -- Textbooks. 2. Bible. Mark -- Study and teaching.
   3. Bible. Mark -- Commentaries.   I. Title. II. Series.

BS2585.55.J63 2017   226.3/07   2016958434

SEEDBED PUBLISHING
Franklin, Tennessee
Seedbed.com

CONTENTS

CONTENTS

CONTENTS

WELCOME TO ONEBOOK: DAILY-WEEKLY

John Wesley, in a letter to one of his leaders, penned the following:

> O begin! Fix some part of every day for private exercises. You may acquire the taste which you have not: what is tedious at first, will afterwards be pleasant.
>
> Whether you like it or not, read and pray daily. It is for your life; there is no other way; else you will be a trifler all your days. . . . Do justice to your own soul; give it time and means to grow. Do not starve yourself any longer. Take up your cross and be a Christian altogether.

Rarely are our lives most shaped by our biggest ambitions and highest aspirations. Rather, our lives are most shaped, for better or for worse, by those small things we do every single day.

At Seedbed, our biggest ambition and highest aspiration is to resource the followers of Jesus to become lovers and doers of the Word of God every single day, to become people of One Book.

To that end, we have created the OneBook Daily-Weekly. First, it's important to understand what this is not: warm, fuzzy, sentimental devotions. If you engage the Daily-Weekly for any length of time, you will learn the Word of God. You will grow profoundly in your love for God, and you will become a passionate lover of people.

How Does the Daily-Weekly Work?

Daily. As the name implies, every day invites a short but substantive engagement with the Bible. Five days a week you will read a passage of Scripture followed by a short segment of teaching and closing with a question for reflection and self-examination. On the sixth day, you will review and reflect on the previous five days.

Weekly. Each week, on the seventh day, find a way to gather with at least one other person doing the study. Pursue the weekly guidance for gathering. Share learning, insight, encouragement, and most importantly, how the Holy Spirit is working in your lives.

That's it. When the twelve weeks are done, we will be ready with twelve more. Four times a year we will release a new edition of the Daily-Weekly. Over time, those who pursue this course of learning will develop a rich library of Bible learning resources for the long haul. Following is the plan for how we will work our way through the Bible.

The Gospels: Twelve weeks of the year the Daily-Weekly will delve into one of the Gospels, either in a broad overview or through a deep dive into a more focused segment of the text.

The Epistles: Twelve weeks of the year the Daily-Weekly will explore one of the letters, sermons, or the Acts of the Apostles that make up the rest of the New Testament.

The Wisdom Writings: Twelve weeks of the year the Daily-Weekly will lead us into some part of the Psalms, Proverbs, or prophetic writings.

The Old Testament: Twelve weeks of the year the Daily-Weekly will engage with some portion of the books of Moses (Genesis–Deuteronomy), the historical books, or other writings from the Old Testament.

If you are looking for a substantive study to learn Scripture through a steadfast method, look no further.

WEEK ONE

Mark 1:1–15

Prologue

INTRODUCTION

The Gospel of Mark is one of four biblical accounts of the life and teaching of Jesus. Written within a generation or so of Jesus himself, Mark's account is the shortest of the four Gospels. It is fast-paced, to the point, and chronicles episodes of Jesus' public life beginning at about age thirty. The Gospel details Jesus' teaching and miracles through the first half of the book. The second half narrows in more precisely on the events leading to his arrest, crucifixion, and resurrection. Because Jesus is the central focus throughout, Mark's Gospel is somewhat biographical. But unlike modern biographies, Mark does not begin with a narration of Jesus' birth and childhood (as do the Gospels of Matthew and Luke). Instead, Mark begins with a rather dramatic prologue.

The use of a dramatic prologue is an age-old practice still in use today. In fact, I remember being surprised as a youth by the opening screen crawl of my first *Star Wars* movie. It was in theaters during its first run in 1977, and much to my surprise the movie (subtitled *Episode IV: A New Hope*) seemed to begin in the middle of things. In a similar way, Mark begins his story in the middle of things with a screen crawl that spans the first fifteen verses of his Gospel. The appearances of John the Baptizer and Jesus in the Judean wilderness are not isolated events on the timeline of history, but part of a much larger saga that is often referred to as "salvation history."

Mark's Gospel is a single episode in God's epic drama. That drama begins in Genesis when God creates the heavens and the earth. It continues through the Old Testament as God's people alternate between periods of obedience and sin. The epic takes a new direction in the four Gospels when Jesus appears on earth to provide victory over sin and death, and it comes to conclusion in Revelation when God creates a new heaven and earth, and banishes death forever. Mark's opening verses are his way of inviting the reader into an epic drama that begins in the middle of things.

ONE

The Beginning of the Gospel

Mark 1:1 *The beginning of the gospel of Jesus Christ, the Son of God.*

Understanding the Word. For years, scholars and commentators on the Gospel of Mark have tried to understand Mark's opening sentence. Does "the beginning of the gospel" refer to the first part of Mark's Gospel, or does the entire account of Jesus' life and ministry as recorded in Mark represent "the beginning of the gospel"?

In the introduction to this week's lessons, I suggested that the first fifteen verses of Mark function as a prologue (or screen crawl) by inviting the reader into the larger story of salvation history. There are good reasons for thinking so. One of those reasons can be found in the opening of Matthew's Gospel. The first verse there reads: "The book of the genealogy of Jesus Christ, the son of David, the son of Abraham." The next sixteen verses list the generations of Jesus from Abraham through David to Jesus, while verse 17 provides an appropriate conclusion to this unit. Matthew's account of Jesus' life and ministry begins in verse 18. Matthew thus begins his Gospel with a prologue.

In a similar way, Mark begins with an introduction, the title of which is, "The beginning of the gospel of Jesus Christ, the Son of God." Why does this matter? It matters because it gives us clues into the writing strategy of Mark and to his reliability as a Gospel writer. Unlike Matthew and John (two of the four Gospel writers), Mark was not one of the twelve disciples whom Jesus chose to accompany him during his years of public ministry. Therefore, Mark was not an eyewitness to the events he reports. Church tradition reveals, however, that Mark was the close companion of Peter, who was not only one of the Twelve but quite arguably their leader. The tradition indicates that Mark carefully recorded what he heard Peter proclaim.

It seems that Mark begins Peter's story at the time in which Peter first encounters Jesus. That meeting comes in Mark 1:16–17, when Jesus calls Peter away from his nets to follow him. Thus, Peter's memoirs begin in verse 16. (We will look at this more closely in next week's lesson.) This presents something of a challenge, though. What might explain the fact that a commercial fisherman would abandon his business interests to follow a traveling, Jewish teacher around the Galilean countryside? Mark has likely penned his introduction (vv. 1–15) at least in part as an explanation for Peter's act: the man who had summoned Peter was the one anticipated by Isaiah hundreds of years earlier and proclaimed by John the Baptizer on the banks of the Jordan River. This was indeed the very Son of God, as the heavenly voice declares in Mark 1:11.

In light of this, we can see how Mark begins with a title for his prologue so as to set it off from Peter's accounts. "The beginning of the gospel" has its origin in the prophetic ministry of Isaiah, continues through the baptizing ministry of John at the Jordan River, and comes to a climax with the advent of Jesus, who is baptized by John, approved by God, tempted by Satan, and introduced in the closing sentence of verses 14–15 as the One who rightly proclaims the coming of God's kingdom.

1. What epic dramas do you recall reading or watching?

2. What role does the opening part of an epic drama play in helping you understand the background to the story?

3. In the instance of Mark, how does the prologue (vv. 1–15) help to set the stage for your encounter with the Gospel?

TWO

True North

Mark 1:2–4 *As it is written in Isaiah the prophet, "Behold, I send my messenger before thy face, who shall prepare thy way; ³the voice of one crying in the wilderness: Prepare the way of the Lord, make his paths straight—"*

⁴John the baptizer appeared in the wilderness, preaching a baptism of repentance for the forgiveness of sins.

Understanding the Word. Throughout his Gospel, Mark places directional cues for his readers as they navigate his text. As we read through Mark, I will highlight some of those cues, many of which come at the beginning. In order for us to find and maintain the course Mark intended, we need to heed his cues carefully from the onset, lest we miss his intended destination. Mark 1:1–15 is just such a directional cue, giving us the background information we need to make sense of a story that begins in the middle of things.

Just as good navigators establish their positions relative to fixed points, Mark makes it clear as early as the second verse that Isaiah represents true north on our journey. Mark's message *must and can only be understood* in light of Isaiah's prophecy. He offers no rationale, no explanation, no justification for this move; he simply does it, and he expects his readers to follow his lead. What, then, might such a move suggest about Mark's intended audience? How would they understand a fixing of the narrative to the point of Isaiah?

In order for us to understand Mark's initial course heading, we must first understand Isaiah. As a major prophet of the Old Testament, Isaiah's message was one of both warning and hope. The *warning* was to a people who had too often redirected their allegiance to human kings instead of their one true King. The consequence of such disobedience is punishment, and God can swing a pretty large paddle. Governed for centuries by its own rotten kings, Israel found itself weakened and under attack by foreign empires. The result was captivity in Babylon. God was exercising his justice, but not from a perspective of vengeance. No, his perspective was love. This is the *hope*. God is faithful to his promises, and was not about to leave his people in such a hopeless state. But salvation could not be offered until the punishment had accomplished its purpose. As the author of the letter to the Hebrews knows, "For the Lord disciplines him whom he loves, and chastises every son whom he receives" (Heb. 12:6). Thus can Isaiah's message be understood as a message of hope. Israel's time of punishment was nearing its end; God was about to send a messenger to proclaim the good news of salvation (see Isaiah 40:9; 52:7).

In some sense, during the time of Jesus God's people were still battling issues of allegiance. Some placed their trust in their works of righteousness. Others placed their trust in the increasingly popular pagan culture. Still others placed their trust in the sword. In each case, God's people were established on a wrong heading, and the role of John the Baptizer was to provide a course corrective through the means of baptism. As the forerunner anticipated by Isaiah, John's work was to prepare the way for the coming King.

The time of John marks a time in which people who walked in darkness saw a great light (see Isaiah 9:2). A period of more than four hundred years stood between the people in John's day and the last written word of Hebrew Scripture. His time marked the conclusion to a long period of agonizing anticipation during which the land of God's people was dominated by pagan, foreign empires.

1. What distracts you from pursuing God? Have you unknowingly pledged your allegiance to that distraction?

2. What is the cost of that false allegiance? Or to put it differently, who is paying the price for your loyalty to that distraction? How much is that price?

3. Who in your life functions as a messenger of either warning or hope? How do you allow such persons to speak forthrightly into your life?

THREE

The Function of a Prophet

Mark 1:5–8 *And there went out to him all the country of Judea, and all the people of Jerusalem; and they were baptized by him in the river Jordan, confessing their sins. ⁶Now John was clothed with camel's hair, and had a leather girdle around his waist, and ate locusts and wild honey. ⁷And he preached, saying, "After me comes he who is mightier than I, the thong of whose sandals I am not worthy to stoop down and untie. ⁸I have baptized you with water; but he will baptize you with the Holy Spirit."*

Understanding the Word. If Mark's first directional cue to his readers is to set their reading in light of Israel's history, his second move seems to narrow the focus to the role of a prophet. Verses 5–8 provide a number of details that highlight both John's seeming peculiarities and his practices.

Mark offers this short narrative about John in very descriptive ways. He seems intent on communicating to the reader important markers for understanding, such as the size of the crowds (*"Everybody* was there!"), the food and clothing details of John, and the surpassing magnitude of the One to come. Why are such details important to Mark? And why—in a world where writing was difficult by modern standards—would Mark waste valuable writing space recounting the dietary and fashion habits of John?

It seems likely that Mark is bringing images to the reader of the Old Testament prophets. Several possible allusions here to Old Testament passages (beyond the explicit reference to Isaiah) strongly suggest that Mark wants his readers to understand John as a prophet of old. These include Malachi 3:1, Exodus 23:20, 2 Kings 1:8, and Zechariah 13:4. How, then, should modern-day interpreters understand such a prophet of old? The answer must come at least in part from an understanding of the nature of the prophetic office.

In the Old Testament accounts, the ongoing role of the prophet was to remind Israel of its one true King: God Almighty. That prophetic role was likely an unpopular one, especially when prophets were called upon to rebuke human kings who acted in their own self-interests rather than pursuing the interests of the true King. The prophet's job was to issue a call to repentance, demanding that God's people surrender their false allegiances and return humbly to their God. John makes it clear that One is coming after him who greatly surpasses John in power and authority. Receiving such a One would require preparation: specifically, a surrendering of unholy allegiances. Although a noble task, fulfilling the mission of a prophet could certainly evoke the wrath of the reigning king. John's work would, in fact, earn him a beheading at the hands of Herod (see Mark 6:17–29). Nevertheless, John appeared publicly in the Judean wilderness, tending to the assembled masses on the banks of the Jordan, preparing themselves for whatever was about to happen next.

But what was the nature of that movement to the Jordan River? Was it the peaceful setting we see in movies, with folks patiently waiting their turns to be gently immersed by a grizzly-looking baptizer speaking with a proper British accent? More likely, the response took the shape of a crisis. People knew that the coming of the One would be a double-edged sword, bringing salvation to the righteous and judgment to the wicked. Recall the words of Isaiah as we read them yesterday. Note how Luke captures that tension in Luke 3:6–7. Even though Isaiah's prophecy (as stated in Luke) suggests that all flesh will see the salvation of God, John the Baptist understood that this would be a word of warning to the proud: "You brood of vipers! Who warned you to flee from the wrath to come?" (Matt. 3:7).

1. If the role of the prophet was to challenge false allegiances, who plays that role in your life today? Should such a role be reserved for our clergy, or does every believer have the right (and responsibility) to speak a word of truth into the life of another believer?

2. What would be the cost of allowing someone to speak a prophetic word of warning into your life today? What would be the cost of *not* allowing such a person to speak such a word?

3. What experience have you had with public acknowledgment of sin? Are you carrying an ongoing sin that you'd like to make known, even to just one other person?

FOUR

The Return of the King

Mark 1:9–13 *In those days Jesus came from Nazareth of Galilee and was baptized by John in the Jordan. [10]And when he came up out of the water, immediately he saw the heavens opened and the Spirit descending upon him like a dove; [11]and a voice came from heaven, "Thou art my beloved Son; with thee I am well pleased."*

[12]The Spirit immediately drove him out into the wilderness. [13]And he was in the wilderness forty days, tempted by Satan; and he was with the wild beasts; and the angels ministered to him.

Understanding the Word. If Mark 1:2–4 is a directional cue to guide our reading with reference to Isaiah, and if verses 5–8 are a more specific cue with regard to understanding John within the tradition of Old Testament prophets, then verses 9–11 provide a further narrowing of directional heading by means of a wording shift. Whereas John was largely in the spotlight in verses 4–8, the primary focus shifts abruptly to Jesus as the main actor in verses 9–15. In effect, the spotlight—which began broadly with Isaiah and narrowed with John—now shifts to Jesus. What is not said in Mark is that John baptized

Jesus. What *is* said in verse 9 is that Jesus "was baptized" by John. Although a seemingly minor grammatical point, the use of the passive voice here is a dramatic way for Mark to make Jesus the central focus as John recedes into the background.

This creates a clear and dramatic contrast. Jesus is both *like* and *unlike* John. If we understand John to operate within a long, prophetic tradition, then we can see Jesus likewise operating within that same tradition. However, John is quick to illustrate the differences between Jesus and himself. The coming One would surpass John's ministry in all ways (and, in fact, the ministries of all the prophets). Not only does Jesus receive divine affirmation when the sky splits, he also successfully faces Satan in the wilderness. But why would Jesus be sent into this barren, dangerous region? Further, how should we understand Jesus' encounter with Satan?

One of the distinctive features of Christianity is the reality of an *incarnational* God, or a God who takes on human flesh to dwell among his people. So far in our reading, we've seen that Jesus seems to come from a normal locale: Nazareth. His background could have been anyone's background. Further, we notice that he submits to baptism at John's hands, just like everyone else. Now we learn that Jesus is subject to temptations . . . again, like we all are. The key difference here is that his temptations are on a scale that really suggests that Jesus is anything but a typical human being. Although Mark is careful to make sure that Jesus is like other persons in many ways, he also makes it clear that Jesus differs from other persons in his relationship to God, bearing the very stamp of divine sonship.

As we consider the reality of Jesus, it's of utmost importance that we remember that Jesus—in ways that are difficult to understand—uniquely and completely balances his human and divine characteristics. Surviving in the wilderness, without food, without water, without shade, and without shelter for forty days would be painful. It would, in fact, be difficult to watch. However, and in spite of the ongoing snares of Satan, Jesus prevails precisely because of God's care for him through the ministry of angels.

In sum, Jesus emerges as the rightful heir to the divine throne precisely because his allegiance to the King is *complete*. Even in the face of Satan's temptations, Jesus remains solidly grounded in his submission and loyalty to the true King.

1. Have you noticed that, up to this point, Mark does not record Jesus as having yet spoken? Why do you suppose Mark would intentionally keep the star of the show silent?

2. Looking back on Mark's opening, Isaiah seems to provide the authorization for John's ministry, and John likewise seems to provide—at least in some measure—the authorization for Jesus' ministry. How do you suppose the declaration of the heavenly voice (v. 11) adds to Jesus' status?

3. As you consider the voices in your life that seem to speak with authority, what is it *specifically* that lends such authority to their voices?

4. How does knowing that Jesus fully identified with humanity impact your confidence in him? How would your faith be different if this temptation narrative were not included in the Gospel?

FIVE

"Repent . . . and Believe!"

Mark 1:14–15 *Now after John was arrested, Jesus came into Galilee, preaching the gospel of God,* *[15]and saying, "The time is fulfilled, and the kingdom of God is at hand; repent, and believe in the gospel."*

Understanding the Word. The idea of "the kingdom of God" is central in this passage. However, our modern understanding of kingship and kingdoms has shifted since the time of Jesus. We tend to think of royalty reigning from palaces, serving as visual symbols of a nation's values and might. To be sure, ancient kingship during the era of Jesus shares some similarities with modern ideas. However, we must have a better sense of kingship in the ancient Near East if we are to more fully understand what Jesus might have meant by his proclamation about the approach of the kingdom of God.

Kingship in the days of Jesus would have carried with it certain historical and cultural assumptions. For instance, most ancient persons would likely have understood that kings were often interested in working cooperatively (in varying degrees) with their subject peoples. An incoming king would invite respect and allegiance by offering the subject people various provisions, like political identity, military protection, and economic stability. In exchange for these provisions, the king would expect (and even demand) that his subjects would contribute to the king's treasury through their earnings or resources. He would expect his subjects to obey his laws, and to provide a fighting force in the service of the king. And perhaps most important, the king would demand *absolute allegiance* from his subjects. Forming alliances and making treaties with other political powers or kingdoms would earn the subjects swift and terrible punishment.

With this understanding of kingship in mind, how might Jesus' message have been received by his hearers? Most likely, they would have heard in Jesus' message an announcement that things were about to change; that there was a new sheriff in town. Further, they would have heard in Jesus' message a word of hope, specifically that this long-awaited kingdom was at hand. Finally, they would have understood that repentance would require a breaking of all other allegiances. Only under such unconditional loyalty would the advancing kingdom be understood as truly good news.

Notice also the order in which Jesus' first two commandments are given. First he issues a call for repentance, and *then* he invites his hearers into belief. A study of the two words for *repent* and *believe* quickly reveals something other than what many Christians today think. Repentance, normally thought of as a change of behavior, actually refers to a change of thought. In the days of Jesus, to repent was often a word used by a surrendering army as it abandoned its position in opposition to the stronger army. To repent would be something like "to surrender" one's commitments, position, or allegiances. In addition, to believe was not simply a matter of what one thought (as it is widely held today), but rather a term that expressed the placing of one's confidence or trust in another. For example, to *believe in* someone or something required one to step out in the confidence that the individual or entity was reliable.

In this way, we see Jesus ushering in the kingdom of God with a simple formula. The first step is to rid oneself of foreign allegiances and false loyalties; in effect, to cleanse one's mind. The second step is to fully trust the King as provider, sustainer, and protector. Only in this way will the full benefit and good news of citizenship in the kingdom be realized.

1. Questions of *allegiance* have been numerous in our study so far. As you read through this week's lessons, what new insights do you have regarding your own allegiances, distractions, and things that might tempt you?

2. When you consider those things, who or what can you turn to for support?

3. In what ways do you find yourself unwilling or unable to fully trust God, even if you're potentially willing to shed other allegiances?

COMMENTARY NOTES

General Comments. The English word "gospel" is used principally in two different ways. On one hand, it refers to a proclamation of good news, and the Greek word *euangelion* on which "gospel" is based (or "godspell" in Old English) gives us the English word "evangelism." The opening of Mark is curious because it could be read in one of two ways: either Mark is documenting the good news *about* Jesus (e.g., that he forgives sins and raises the dead), or he is documenting the good news *from* Jesus (e.g., announcing that "the time has been fulfilled and the kingdom of God is at hand"). It's also possible that Mark means both at the same time. On the other hand, "gospel" came to refer to a written account of the life of Jesus. We have four Gospels in this sense in our New Testament: those of Mathew, Mark, Luke, and John. Titles were later added to each Gospel to distinguish them from one another, and each was referenced as *The Gospel According to X*, where *X* represents the name of the Gospel writer. In the case of Mark, the title of his work became *KATA MARKON* (that is, "according to Mark"). As with other commentaries on the New Testament, I'll distinguish the gospel (the good news about and/or from Jesus) from the Gospel (the written account of Mark) by means of upper- and lower-case letters: gospel versus Gospel.

General Comments. Although most versions of Mark's Gospel conclude at 16:20, the earliest available manuscripts (i.e., handwritten documents) conclude Mark abruptly at 16:8. It seems that some have made attempts to provide more suitable endings to Mark, but they are most likely not original to Mark's pen.

Day 4. Why is it important to note this change of focus? Recall that John reported that the coming One would: come *after* John; be *of greater magnitude* than John; and baptize *in the future* and with the *Holy Spirit* (Mark 1:7).

Day 4. When the region of "the wilderness" is mentioned in the prologue, we probably ought to dismiss any notions of a forest or deep woods, for the wilderness as it is referred to here was more likely a dry, desert-like region. The sense of the underlying Greek word is a desolate, uninhabitable place. It was the abode of bandits who would assault defenseless travelers. It was the place for wild and dangerous animals. It lacked water and shelter. But perhaps most important, it was often the stage where spiritual warfare took place. Palestine, as the setting for the life and events of Jesus, consisted of a variety of regions. The mountainous ridge on which Jerusalem sits, the deep valley of the Jordan River basin, and the slowly rising flatlands of the coastal regions all contribute in some way to the landscape of the Holy Land. But perhaps no region is more packed with significance than the "wilderness," and Mark skillfully orients his readers to that locale through several references to wild places and things (vv. 3–4, 6, 12–13). Such a concentration of words related to the *wild* occurs nowhere else in Mark. The Greek word is *erēmos*.

WEEK ONE

GATHERING DISCUSSION OUTLINE

A. Open session in prayer. Ask for specific celebrations of God's goodness.

B. What new insights have you gained from this week's readings? What has encouraged you? What has challenged you?

C. View video for this week's readings.

D. Discuss questions selected from daily readings.

1. **KEY OBSERVATION:** The Gospel of Mark begins with a dramatic prologue.

    DISCUSSION QUESTION: In what areas (literature, film, etc.) have you encountered prologues? Name some examples. What is their function? How might Mark 1:1–15 set the stage for the drama about to unfold?

2. **KEY OBSERVATION:** Isaiah represents true north for Mark.

    DISCUSSION QUESTION: What do you know about Isaiah? How might an understanding of the message of Isaiah help Mark's reader to better understand the message of his Gospel?

3. **KEY OBSERVATION:** John the Baptizer was a prophet in the tradition of Isaiah.

    DISCUSSION QUESTION: When you consider the term *prophet*, what images come to mind? What attributes do prophets typically have?

How did John the Baptizer demonstrate those attributes? Why is it important to see John within the tradition of Old Testament prophets?

4. **KEY OBSERVATION:** Jesus emerges as the legitimate heir to the kingdom of God on earth.

   DISCUSSION QUESTION: In what ways is Jesus Christ the King? How does an understanding of kingship in his day affect our understanding of his lordship today?

5. **KEY OBSERVATION:** Allegiance to God's kingdom requires repentance and belief.

   DISCUSSION QUESTION: How does the video challenge your ideas about *repentance* and *belief*? What allegiances do you or your congregation need to abandon in order to more fully make room for the kingdom of God? What is the price of trusting Jesus as Lord?

E. What facts and information presented in the commentary portion of the lesson help you understand the weekly Scripture?

F. Close session with prayer. Ask for specific concerns to be brought before our Lord.

WEEK TWO

Mark 1:16–45

Uncommon Authority

INTRODUCTION

The message and ministry of Jesus is as uncommon a message today as it was in his own day. Too often the preaching we hear from our pulpits relates to *what* we should believe or *how* we should believe, but it in so many ways seems to lack the power to result in real transformation. And by *transformation*, I mean to say a return to the glory of God with which we were originally created.

God's work in salvation history is an effort to awaken his people from their spiritual numbness so that they can turn and be healed. This is the process of salvation. We tend to think of being saved as a decision or prayer that we make as a way of securing for ourselves a place in eternity with Jesus. In reality, Jesus ushered in the era of salvation when he came to this earth. Some say that Jesus came to turn the world upside down. In reality, he came to turn it right-side up.

One of the main reasons why I am so completely comfortable in the company of Wesleyans (whether they be members of the Wesleyan church, Free Methodist, United Methodist, Nazarene, or any other of a number of sister denominations) is because John Wesley helps me see that salvation begins in the here and now. Mark chronicles Jesus' mighty works on earth, many of which were directly related to restoring people to the fullness of life God intended for them. Whether you're a leper, suffering from a mental disorder, or lying in bed with a fever, salvation is available *here . . . and now.*

For Wesley, salvation means returning to life as God intended it in Genesis 1–2. Sure, that involves spending eternity with Jesus. But it means more than that. It means spending *today* with Jesus. Throughout this week's lessons, pay particularly close attention to how Jesus restores persons to their full humanity and, in so doing, brings salvation.

ONE
The Testimony of Witnesses

Mark 1:16–20 *And passing along by the Sea of Galilee, he saw Simon and Andrew the brother of Simon casting a net in the sea; for they were fishermen.* *[17]And Jesus said to them, "Follow me and I will make you become fishers of men." [18]And immediately they left their nets and followed him. [19]And going on a little farther, he saw James the son of Zeb'edee and John his brother, who were in their boat mending the nets. [20]And immediately he called them; and they left their father Zeb'edee in the boat with the hired servants, and followed him.*

Understanding the Word. In today's society, we have the technology to record everything from bank transactions to phone conversations; from football games to home movies; from satellite images to text messages. In sum, we have an unprecedented capacity to record and preserve the present. Writing history—so to speak—is cheap and easy.

Mark's society was not at all that way. Writing was a difficult and expensive process. Few were literate enough to read and write text. Further, writing materials were in short supply. For instance, a typical writing surface during Mark's day was a sheet of papyrus in which stalks of papyrus plants were split lengthwise, mashed flat, aligned side-by-side with others, then glued together. A second layer was attached to the first, but lying crosswise. The two were joined together to make a sturdier sheet, and the sheet was bleached in the sun. This was a labor-intensive process.

Why does this matter? The words we have recorded in the Bible were carefully chosen. Likewise, the episodes and events that are reported were carefully selected. Not everything could be included the way that today's webcams and smartphones can record trivial information and broadcast it through social media to millions. Mark had no "backspace" key available to him, so whatever we have in his Gospel *matters*.

The insertion of Jesus' calling of the first four disciples in some ways is out of place. The narrative does not flow neatly around verses 16–20. However,

Mark has included it on purpose. Why? The call of the disciples, and the naming of them, lends credibility to Mark's report, for at the time of his writing, most of the twelve apostles were still alive and available to confirm the events surrounding Jesus' life. By listing the four disciples at this stage, Mark indicates that he is a witness to their testimony, especially Peter's.

In a related way, we learn how Peter came to know Jesus. I mentioned in last week's lesson that church history indicates that Mark was Peter's recording secretary of sorts. The calling of the four disciples is a critical piece in the narrative because it marks the beginning of Peter's recollections. Although this week's passages are full of Jesus' miracles and the responses by the ever-growing crowds, verses 16–20 arguably mark the first mighty work of Jesus (the calling of his disciples) and the faithful responses of those he called.

1. What are your earliest impressions of the Bible? What thought did you give to where or when it was written?

2. How important is it for the Bible to be historically accurate and reliable? How does your reading of Mark at this point impact your confidence in his Gospel's historical reliability?

3. What role do you think human authors play in writing inspired Scripture?

TWO

The Evidence of Miracles

Mark 1:21–28 *And they went into Caper′na-um; and immediately on the sabbath he entered the synagogue and taught. ²²And they were astonished at his teaching, for he taught them as one who had authority, and not as the scribes. ²³And immediately there was in their synagogue a man with an unclean spirit; ²⁴and he cried out, "What have you to do with us, Jesus of Nazareth? Have you come to destroy us? I know who you are, the Holy One of God." ²⁵But Jesus rebuked him, saying, "Be silent, and come out of him!" ²⁶And the unclean spirit, convulsing him and crying with a loud voice, came out of him. ²⁷And they were all amazed, so that they questioned among themselves, saying, "What is this? A new teaching! With authority he commands even the unclean spirits, and* *they obey him." ²⁸And at once his fame spread everywhere throughout all the surrounding region of Galilee.*

Understanding the Word. Have you ever heard any of these expressions? "Talk is cheap." "Practice what you preach." "Speak softly, and carry a big stick." "Your actions are so loud I can't hear what you're saying."

Each of them, in its own way, points to a truth: actions speak louder than words. That was especially true in the time of Mark. His world was an interesting blend of Greek (in fact, Mark wrote in Greek) and Jewish influences. One of the characteristics of Greek culture was a commitment to knowing truth through human wisdom. Logical arguments were the way to demonstrate that something was true, or good, or beautiful. Jewish culture was a bit different. For Jews, truth was discerned through evidence. We've already encountered one of those forms of evidence, that of witnesses. Another form of evidence that can prove something true or valid is the performance of a mighty act, or miracle.

Paul notes this distinction in 1 Corinthians 1:22 when he writes, "For Jews demand signs and Greeks seek wisdom." In today's passage, Jesus backs up his powerful preaching with an even more powerful act: he exorcises a demon from a member of the congregation. Now, lest we conjure up images of *The Exorcist* or *Poltergeist*, we need to understand that this event may not have the Hollywood special effects that we've come to expect from exorcisms in film today. Regardless of how it happened, what remains evident in Mark's account is the fact that Jesus restored the man to cleanness, which means right standing within his congregation and community.

It may have been the case that the demoniac was a regular attender of synagogue worship up until that point, with his underlying condition largely undetected by those of his community. It is even more likely that Jesus' teaching was the cause that provoked the demon to speak out. What seem undeniable, based on our reading of this passage, are three things. First, the demoniac's outburst was *disruptive* to the regular pattern of worship. Jesus responds immediately by putting an end to the disruption. Second, the demoniac's utterance was *confused*. Note especially how the demoniac alternates between references to himself as "I" and "we." Third, Jesus' teaching brought the demon out of *hiddenness*. This is the work that Jesus came to do: to restore order, to create clarity, and to shine light in the shadows of life.

Jesus' teaching stands in contrast to that of the scribes (more on them later) precisely because it is backed up by action. This plays very well in a Jewish crowd, and explains in part why the congregation responded with such enthusiasm. Jesus' following grows beyond the first four disciples as his fame begins to spread across the countryside. And note that it is not simply that Jesus performs a miracle; the mighty work he does here restores a man to whole and fruitful living. This man experiences the beginning of salvation.

1. What "proofs" have you encountered that lend support to your belief in God and the claims of the Bible?

2. As you think about your own unique personality, what proofs are more convincing to you? Are you persuaded by logical arguments, or do you prefer evidence of witnesses, miracles, and such?

3. Reflect on this episode of the demoniac in the Capernaum synagogue. Have you ever experienced or witnessed a spiritual manifestation like the one Mark describes for us? How can believers distinguish between unclean spirits and genuine movements of the Holy Spirit? How do proofs help us in that process?

THREE
Healing "Less Than" Existence

Mark 1:29–31 *And immediately he left the synagogue, and entered the house of Simon and Andrew, with James and John.* *³⁰Now Simon's mother-in-law lay sick with a fever, and immediately they told him of her.* *³¹And he came and took her by the hand and lifted her up, and the fever left her; and she served them.*

Understanding the Word. In yesterday's lesson, we briefly talked about whole and fruitful living. In so many cases people live their lives in ways that fail to fully reflect the fact that they are created in the image of God. In fact, we all fail to fully live into that image. This is a result of the fall, when sin entered the world through the errors of Adam and Eve in Genesis 3.

In this story of the healing of Peter's mother-in-law, we note a number of things. First, Peter must have been married at the time of the event or some time previous. Second, it is still the Sabbath. Third, the four witnesses of (Simon) Peter, Andrew, James, and John are present, lending eyewitness testimony to the event. Fourth, Jesus appears to have authority not just over unclean spirits, but over physical illness as well. What strikes me most about this passage, though, is a fifth observation: Peter's mother-in-law *served them* once the fever left her.

Again remembering that Mark wrote in a world where pen and papyrus were in limited supply (and thus everything he wrote matters), why would Mark include such a detail without further explanation? And why would he end this scene at this point?

Mark often ends his scenes with small climaxes, or punctuated points. These endings serve to carry the main thrust or point of the scene. Note how the opening prologue we examined in 1:1–15 ends with a climax: the moment the true King speaks for the first time in Mark's Gospel. In today's Scripture reading, the larger point may not be that Jesus seems to miraculously heal Peter's mother-in-law, but rather that *she was able to serve them.*

But how could *serving* possibly be the main point?

Remember that Jesus appeared in the synagogue teaching with uncommon authority. Remember also that his actions backed up his preaching, and that those actions involved restoring a man to cleanness, or right standing within his religious community. Further, he was restored to his right mind, more fully reflecting the image of God original to him rather than living in the disruption and confusion of his demon possession.

In this passage, we need to understand a bit about Jewish culture, and specifically the way persons maintained roles within a household structure. In a Jewish home, the mother would oversee the daily care and administration of the household. This role would include the offering of hospitality. Women would likely take great pride in their hospitality, and a woman's status in her community would be tied to her ability to offer appropriate hospitality to guests. That Peter's mother-in-law was unable to offer appropriate hospitality to her guests demonstrates that she is not able to live into her potential status, and as a result, she is living life at a "less than" level.

Jesus' healing of her fever impacted her more than in a mere physical sense. It impacted her social standing and restored her dignity. This is what Jesus came to do, and Mark punctuates the scene with this important conclusion.

1. Have you ever missed out on a once-in-a-lifetime event or opportunity because you were sick or otherwise unable to attend? What was the circumstance?

2. How differently would this story have read if Mark had not included the last line, "and she served them"? How important is it to understand the social context of women's status and hospitality during the time of Jesus?

3. In what areas of life is illness, shame, or other circumstances robbing you of human dignity? Are you willing to ask Jesus, who healed Peter's mother-in-law, to heal you?

FOUR

A Hard Day's Night

Mark 1:32–39 *That evening, at sundown, they brought to him all who were sick or possessed with demons. ³³And the whole city was gathered together about the door. ³⁴And he healed many who were sick with various diseases, and cast out many demons; and he would not permit the demons to speak, because they knew him.*

³⁵And in the morning, a great while before day, he rose and went out to a lonely place, and there he prayed. ³⁶And Simon and those who were with him pursued him, ³⁷and they found him and said to him, "Every one is searching for you." ³⁸And he said to them, "Let us go on to the next towns, that I may preach there also; for that is why I came out." ³⁹And he went throughout all Galilee, preaching in their synagogues and casting out demons.

Understanding the Word. One of the things that interpreters of Mark's Gospel have noted is a tendency by Mark to speak in doublets; that is, a restatement of what he has just said. In this passage, he seems to be doing just that by saying, "That evening, *at sundown . . .*" I wonder, though, if Mark is really speaking in a doublet here or if, in fact, he is offering us another cue.

In our world, we think of Sabbath as being Sunday. In Mark's time, Sabbath was actually Saturday, or more precisely, from sundown on Friday to sundown on Saturday. We note that the preceding events (the teaching in the Capernaum synagogue, the healing of the man with an unclean spirit, the curing of Peter's mother-in-law of her fever) all occur on Sabbath. I suspect what Mark is indicating here is that the Sabbath has officially ended. Though it is the same day (likely Saturday), Sabbath ended at sunset. (We'll discuss Mark's treatment of time in greater detail in Week 11.)

Why would this be an important detail?

It indicates that the city does not gather around Jesus for healing until Sabbath had ended. This likely suggests that the townspeople of Capernaum did not want to bring their sick to Jesus during the Sabbath because it would violate the Jewish law in terms of Sabbath regulations. A whole host of laws existed in regard to the proper keeping of Sabbath, and Jews were careful to observe all those laws. There were even laws that governed how many steps a person could take on Sabbath without violating it.

Jesus seems to be above those laws in these stories, for he performs healings without any seeming concern for the law. Although the townspeople are unwilling to violate those laws themselves, they seem unconcerned that Jesus is doing so. In fact, Mark notes the response of the people to Jesus' healing ministry as being extraordinary. Truly a great One was in their midst. The healings must have lasted well into the night, for Mark reports Jesus as rising and slipping away from their midst. The crowd was likely still on hand some time later since Mark reports that some were looking for him. Jesus had to be absolutely exhausted. After all, messiahship is hard work.

But what about the ending of this scene? Note that Mark concludes by saying that Jesus' mission required him to go into the surrounding towns. His message and work of healing wasn't restricted to a limited number of people. Rather, it was made available to all. Perhaps one of the reasons that Jesus silenced the demons (and, as we will soon see, silences humans, as well) is because he knew that the message would spread quickly, and his ability to freely go from town to town would be hampered. We will see numerous instances of this exact outcome in the coming scenes, and most certainly in tomorrow's lesson.

1. Jesus seems to violate the Sabbath in these passages, and thus breaks religious law. What might Mark be trying to tell us here?

2. What is your view of Sabbath? How have you arrived at that view? Are you satisfied with your observance of weekly rest?

3. What obstacles stand in the way of experiencing *true* rest each week? What guidelines do you use in determining what is appropriate with regard to Sabbath activities?

FIVE

The Loose Lips of a Leper

Mark 1:40–45 *And a leper came to him beseeching him, and kneeling said to him, "If you will, you can make me clean." ⁴¹Moved with pity, he stretched out his hand and touched him, and said to him, "I will; be clean." ⁴²And immediately the leprosy left him, and he was made clean. ⁴³And he sternly charged him, and sent him away at once, ⁴⁴and said to him, "See that you say nothing to any one; but go, show yourself to the priest, and offer for your cleansing what Moses commanded, for a proof to the people." ⁴⁵But he went out and began to talk freely about it, and to spread the news, so that Jesus could no longer openly enter a town, but was out in the country; and people came to him from every quarter.*

Understanding the Word. In Mark's world, having an infectious disease like leprosy required a person to isolate him- or herself from others. It was in effect a banishment to exile, resulting in a "less than" existence.

Apparently, this particular leper somehow got word of Jesus' ability to heal the sick and made a very bold move by approaching Jesus. That Jesus touched him was completely unthinkable, for such contact not only posed the risk of contracting the disease, but it would have placed Jesus with the leper as a banned person. Jesus nullified that likely verdict when he instantly healed the man of his leprous condition, restoring him to an appropriate status within the community.

Note what follows the healing: Jesus directs the man to present himself to the priest and offer the appropriate gift pursuant to the law. Why? Because Jesus knew that this would prove to people that Jesus was a law-abiding Jew.

In his enthusiasm (and one can hardly doubt that the healed man rejoiced over his healing), the man goes about the town broadcasting the news. We ourselves would probably do likewise. Who wouldn't? But the man violated a direct order from Jesus *not* to spread the news. Why would Jesus command the man to silence? We've already addressed this a bit in a preceding lesson, where Jesus commanded the demons to remain silent. Mark actually gives us the reason for the command to silence. The man's loose lips resulted in a circumstance in which Jesus' popularity hindered his freedom to move about the countryside: "But he went out and began to talk freely about it, and to spread the news, *so that* Jesus could no longer openly enter a town, but was out in the country" (v. 45, emphasis added).

What was the price for the leper's disobedience? It was that Jesus' ministry was hindered. News traveled so quickly that the crowds actually became an obstacle to Jesus' ability to freely come and go as he needed. Throughout this first chapter of Mark, we see Jesus' popularity growing, slowly at first with the four disciples, but gaining momentum with each successive scene. The presence and role of the crowds in Mark's Gospel is significant, and those crowds will unwittingly serve to provoke the opponents of Jesus, who ultimately orchestrate Jesus' arrest and condemnation.

1. Yesterday we asked questions about Jesus' observance of the Sabbath and, specifically, his seeming disregard for the law. How does today's passage change your view, if at all, of Jesus' relationship to the law? (You may want to skip ahead in our study to read Mark 2:23–28.)

2. If faced with the command to maintain silence, how difficult would it be for you to obey if Jesus miraculously healed you of leprosy or some other awful condition?

3. In what ways do you get ahead of God by taking matters into your own hands? Do you ever rationalize a decision or action that accomplishes (in your mind) some sort of good despite the fact that it violates a biblical principle or command?

COMMENTARY NOTES

Day 1. The words *apostle* and *disciple* can be a bit confusing. A *disciple* is a student or follower of another person. An *apostle* is someone who is sent, dispatched, or commissioned to act on someone else's behalf. The twelve disciples specifically chosen by Jesus are often referred to as "apostles" because they became firsthand eyewitnesses to and representatives of Jesus' ministry and teaching. Later in the New Testament, Paul is also referred to as an apostle because Jesus appeared to him in a vision and called him to go to the Gentiles (or, "non-Jews") to proclaim the gospel.

Day 1. Most Christians believe that the Bible is the inspired word of God. What they mean by "inspired," however, is open to debate. On one hand, many believe that God guided the pens of the Bible's human authors, *dictating* to them what they should write in a word-for-word fashion. According to this view, the role of the human author is unimportant. On the other hand, some believe that the Bible is a product of human encounters with God, and as such, represents their best recollections, impressions, and experiences of God and his work in the world. According to this view, the human author is of primary concern.

The term *inspired* means "breathed into." The word appears prominently in 2 Timothy 3:16, where Paul writes that "All scripture is inspired by God [*God-breathed*]." The challenge of applying this definition of inspiration to the whole of the Bible is that much of the New Testament wasn't yet written when Paul wrote his letter to Timothy. This raises important questions about the ways we should understand the idea of inspiration.

Probably the healthiest view of inspiration is found with the *plenary verbal inspiration* theory. According to this view, God operated through the Holy Spirit to ensure that the human authors chose words that accurately and faithfully reflect God's intent throughout the whole of the Bible. The strength of this view is that we can see the importance of both God as the divine author and humans as earthly authors. In some cases, God speaks directly and the words we have in the original languages of Scripture are original to God (such as in Exodus 31:18). In other cases, we have human agents operating under the guidance of the Holy Spirit to provide trustworthy instruction regarding matters of faith and practice. First Corinthians 7:25 is a great example of this. The point is that we, as faithful interpreters of Scripture, need to understand the role of context as we read.

Day 3. Sometimes the apostle Peter is referred to as simply Peter, sometimes Simon, and sometimes Simon Peter. The name Simon (or, *Simōn* in Greek) is most likely Peter's given name. However, in Matthew 16:18, Jesus says to Simon, "You are Peter, and on this rock I will build my church, and the powers of death shall not prevail against it." Here, Jesus uses the Greek word *petros* (meaning, "rock") to give Simon a new name. That name becomes Peter in English. Aramaic (the native tongue of Jesus) uses the word *kēphas* for "rock," and thus the name Cephas for Simon Peter appears in John 1:42 and elsewhere.

WEEK TWO

GATHERING DISCUSSION OUTLINE

A. Open session in prayer. Ask for specific celebrations of God's goodness.

B. What new insights have you gained from this week's readings? What has encouraged you? What has challenged you?

C. View video for this week's readings.

D. Discuss questions selected from daily readings.

1. **KEY OBSERVATION:** Mark's attention to detail lends historical reliability to his account.

   DISCUSSION QUESTION: What is the role of faith in reading the Bible? Is faith strengthened or weakened by historical reality and evidence? What role do you think historical evidence should play in a believer's faith?

2. **KEY OBSERVATION:** Jesus' mighty works stood in sharp contrast to the religious leaders' empty words.

   DISCUSSION QUESTION: How would you characterize the pulpit preaching you have heard in churches you've attended? Does it demonstrate power that transforms people and congregations? If so, how? If not, why not?

3. **KEY OBSERVATION:** Jesus' mighty works saved people from "less than" existence.

DISCUSSION QUESTION: If someone asked you, "Are you saved?" or, "Have you been saved?" how would you respond? What does "saved" mean in today's Christian world? How does your reading of Mark 1 impact your understanding of salvation (if at all)?

4. **KEY OBSERVATION:** Jesus' mighty works drew huge crowds.

   DISCUSSION QUESTION: Compare Mark's account in Mark 1 with any knowledge of or experience you've had with "faith healers." How are they similar? How are they different? How does Mark's portrait of Jesus affect your view?

5. **KEY OBSERVATION:** The enthusiasm of the crowds hindered Jesus' freedom to conduct his ministry.

   DISCUSSION QUESTION: In what ways do we get in the way of ministry today? Are the ministries we're involved in hampered because of our enthusiasm? Or are our ministries more hampered by our apathy? If so, how?

E. What other facts and information presented in the commentary portion of the lesson help you understand the weekly Scripture?

F. Close session with prayer. Ask for specific concerns to be brought before our Lord.

WEEK THREE

Mark 2:1–3:35

Early Opposition

INTRODUCTION

You would think that everyone would rally around the fact that God showed up in human form to restore the world and its people to their original and intended natures. Healing the sick, delivering amazing sermons, silencing demons: this is all stuff that everyone ought to be excited about.

But as we move through Mark's narrative, trouble begins lurking in the waters, for there are some who find in Jesus a threat to their own understandings of right and wrong, of truth and falsehood. The tide begins to turn in these passages as Jesus is increasingly confronted by and responds to challenges from the religious scholars (scribes) and leaders (Pharisees). The challenges start in very subtle ways, but increase the more Jesus presents a challenge to the existing religious rules and structures.

When Jesus arrives on the public scene, he does so in ways that go against the expectations of the religious insiders. Jesus doesn't fit their mold of what a Messiah should look and act like. He claims authority that no mere mortal should claim. He violates their notions of Sabbath-keeping. And he cavorts with sinners. In fact, Jesus is so ill-suited to their expectations that the religious leaders can only reject both him and his message. Fortunately, Jesus' message is not stopped by the scribes and the Pharisees. It seems that with each attempt to stifle Jesus, the flames of enthusiasm for his mission and ministry are only further kindled.

We will see that God's concern for his people goes ahead of his people. It is universally available. It is unconditional. It is found in the work of others. It is found in the hands of Jesus. It is found in a word of rebuke. And it is found in the forgiveness of our sins. Mark will show us how God—through Jesus—offers a grace that is far deeper and wider than we can possibly imagine . . . a grace so big that some might find it a bit unacceptable.

ONE

Desperate Measures

Mark 2:1–5 *And when he returned to Caper'na-um after some days, it was reported that he was at home. ²And many were gathered together, so that there was no longer room for them, not even about the door; and he was preaching the word to them. ³And they came, bringing to him a paralytic carried by four men. ⁴And when they could not get near him because of the crowd, they removed the roof above him; and when they had made an opening, they let down the pallet on which the paralytic lay. ⁵And when Jesus saw their faith, he said to the paralytic, "My son, your sins are forgiven."*

Understanding the Word. Even though Jesus explicitly ordered the cleansed leper to tell no one what had happened to him (Mark 1:44), the leper nevertheless broadcast the news. As a result of the leper's disobedient act, Jesus was no longer free to move from city to city. For a period of "some days," he remains in the Galilean countryside (2:1). At the end of this period of days, Jesus returns to his home where he can sleep in his own bed, but even here his presence cannot be hidden. Despite his attempts to avoid the public eye, the crowds nevertheless find him.

Word leaks out that Jesus has returned home, and people once again begin thronging around him. Mark tells us that Jesus "was preaching the word" to them. Although we can't know for sure what the word was, it was likely the same word that Jesus spoke to the leper in 1:41: "Be clean." In other words, Jesus was likely performing the same kinds of miraculous healings and providing the same kinds of marvelous teaching that he had been doing since his arrival in Capernaum, and with the same effect of attracting throngs of people (see Mark 1:32–34). The people respond by converging on his home in such large measure that they are no longer able to enter the house.

The Greek text suggests that they were no longer able to move, not even those at the door. This scene reminds us of the one at Peter's and Andrew's home, where Jesus healed Peter's mother-in-law. In that scene, the "whole city was gathered together about the door" (1:33). The scene in today's reading is a bit different, though. The response is greater and the crowd presses more urgently upon Jesus. People can no longer enter and exit the building. A mob mentality emerges as a logjam of human flesh develops at the house, unwittingly creating two classes of people: those within the house who sit within view and earshot of Jesus' deeds and words, and those outside the house who feverishly press in to get a glimpse of this homegrown miracle worker. The insiders hoard Jesus' teaching, while those on the outside remain powerless to reach him. The obstacle is the house. How ironic that the structure intended to provide a safe place for Jesus to rest becomes a structure that creates insiders and outsiders.

When Jesus' house becomes an obstacle to outsiders, the stretcher-carriers dismantle it. It is curious that Jesus raises no objections to the perseverance of those four stretcher-carriers. We don't hear Jesus say to them, "Hey! You're messing up my roof!" or "That's going to cost you!" or "You'll be hearing from my lawyer!" Instead, Jesus takes the occasion not only to heal the man of his paralysis, but also to forgive him of his sins. Jesus restores the man to wholeness. Jesus welcomes the paralytic into his home.

In eighteenth-century England, John Wesley recognized the need to take the message of Jesus to the people rather than requiring the people to come to Jesus within the walls of a church building or the boundaries of a particular parish jurisdiction. He is famous for declaring, "I look upon all the world as my parish." Like Jesus, Wesley understood the need to proclaim the gospel "outside the walls."

1. As you consider your own local church, would you characterize it as a place that nurtures insiders, a place that reaches outsiders, or somewhere between the two?

2. What *specific* evidence can you point to that would support your characterization above? Consider, for example, church ministries, programs, budget allocations, etc.

3. What role do you play in your church's commitment to reaching outsiders? How does Wesley's example encourage or convict you personally with regard to reaching outsiders?

TWO

Actions Speak Louder Than Words

Mark 2:6–11 *Now some of the scribes were sitting there, questioning in their hearts, [7]"Why does this man speak thus? It is blasphemy! Who can forgive sins but God alone?" [8]And immediately Jesus, perceiving in his spirit that they thus questioned within themselves, said to them, "Why do you question thus in your hearts? [9]Which is easier, to say to the paralytic, 'Your sins are forgiven,' or to say, 'Rise, take up your pallet and walk'? [10]But that you may know that the Son of man has authority on earth to forgive sins"—he said to the paralytic—[11]"I say to you, rise, take up your pallet and go home."*

Understanding the Word. It's curious that Jesus, upon seeing the newly made hole in his roof and a cripple being lowered through it, does not address what seems to be the immediate concern: the paralysis of the man. Instead, Mark records that Jesus, once he sees the faith of the stretcher-carriers, declares that the paralytic's sins are forgiven. Of course Jesus is concerned with the man's physical well-being, as we shall soon see. However, the more pressing concern is the condition of his relationship to God. In declaring the man's sins forgiven, Jesus captures this occasion as an opportunity to reveal something about his identity: he claims authority that only God himself can rightly claim.

As you'll recall, John the Baptizer arrived on the scene in 1:4 as one who proclaimed a baptism of repentance for the forgiveness of sins, but there it may be the case that John understood his role as a mediator; God was ultimately the one who provided the forgiveness. Likewise, the Jerusalem temple priests maintained authority to forgive sins, but their authority was based on God's acceptance of the sinner's offering. Like John the Baptist, the priests acted as mediators while God was the final authority for forgiving sins.

In today's reading, Jesus does something a bit unexpected: he declares the paralytic forgiven without mediating a baptism, a sacrifice, or a ritual offering. He declares the man forgiven on the basis of Jesus' own authority, a declaration that can only be understood as some sort of claim of divinity.

Inside the house, scribes (religious experts) are on hand. They are probably there to provide eyewitness testimony to the religious establishment regarding the activities of this travelling miracle worker. They are, in reality, merely taking up seats in the house that could have been otherwise taken by folks in need. They are insiders blocking access to Jesus. When Jesus declares the paralytic forgiven, the scribes are disturbed. Such a self-claim could only be understood as blasphemy. This scene establishes a pattern of challenges to Jesus' authority that will only increase as we move forward in Mark's second chapter. With each successive account, the challenges become greater and more direct. Scholars call these collective episodes in Mark's second chapter "controversy stories." In this first instance, the challenge begins quietly with the religious leaders questioning Jesus' authority internally among themselves.

Jesus, with supernatural hearing, picks up on their murmurings and calls them out. Forgiving sins in *word* is easy; anyone can do that. However, healing a man's body in *deed* is another matter altogether. In order to demonstrate his authority to forgive sins (and, in effect, his *divine* authority), Jesus does what only a divine agent could do: he performs a miracle before the eyes of his challengers. Such miracles serve an important function in Mark's Gospel because they demonstrate Jesus' divine status. These "mighty works" are rendered in Greek by the word *dynameis*, a word that is closely related to the English word *dynamite*. Like dynamite, Jesus' mighty works really pack a punch. For some, such works are marvelous and wonderful, as 2:12 reports: "they were all amazed and glorified God, saying, 'We never saw anything like this!'" For others, however, Jesus' mighty works were frightening, intimidating, and even threatening.

1. Notice that Jesus never makes a self-claim about his divine status. He alludes to it, but he doesn't come right out and say it. Why do you suppose he avoids such a self-declaration?

2. What do you suppose Jesus means by "Son of man" when he apparently refers to himself in 2:10?

3. How important is Jesus' mighty work in this passage to your understanding of Jesus' true identity? Would you understand the passage any differently if Mark had not reported Jesus' healing of the paralytic?

THREE

Sinner Dinner

Mark 2:15–17 *And as he sat at table in his house, many tax collectors and sinners were sitting with Jesus and his disciples; for there were many who followed him. [16]And the scribes of the Pharisees, when they saw that he was eating with sinners and tax collectors, said to his disciples, "Why does he eat with tax collectors and sinners?" [17]And when Jesus heard it, he said to them, "Those who are well have no need of a physician, but those who are sick; I came not to call the righteous, but sinners."*

Understanding the Word. Jesus makes an enormous point in this passage, one that perhaps surprises everyone. He goes looking for the lost. His grace precedes their ability to "get right with the Lord." His fellowship, his love, his mercy, his healing, and his *grace* are available 24/7 . . . anytime, anywhere. There is nowhere that a woman can go to escape the undeniable fact that God loves her. There is nowhere that a man can hide and still escape the undeniable fact that God loves him. God's love and grace are available to *all*. Wesley called this *prevenient* grace, because it exists before we even respond.

Levi (whom we also know as "Matthew," or the author of the first Gospel) is a case in point. As a tax collector, he would have been one of the outsiders with regard to the Jewish community. Most would have seen him as a traitor, one who has sold out his own people for the opportunity to make a living (most likely through dishonest means) collecting taxes from his fellow Jews. Yet Jesus invited him into service. Unthinkable.

Much of Jesus' conflict with the religious establishment arose precisely because of his insistence on bringing good news to those who most needed it. He was willing to get his hands dirty by hanging out with the smokers, the drinkers, the partiers, the sleazy, the foul-mouthed, the cheaters, the scoundrels, and any other sort of vice-loving person within earshot. Jesus met them where they were, but he wasn't willing to leave them there.

Coming to Jesus requires nothing in advance . . . no payment, no dress code, no membership status. It requires *nothing* . . . except a willingness to submit to his lordship. And that submission is a little bit like going to boot camp.

First, he's going to break us down. That involves surrendering false allegiances, especially to self. Then he's going to build us up. That involves reclaiming the image of God that we were created to bear. It is true that membership has its privileges, but it's also true that membership has its responsibilities. Some want the privileges of being a Christ-follower, so they accept Jesus as *Savior*, but they don't want the responsibilities, so they fail to let him reign as *Lord*. Jesus invites, and *requires*, that we accept him as both.

In today's episode, Mark reports this about the sinners and tax collectors: *there were many who followed him* (v. 15). Jesus is developing a following, and that following does not escape the notice of the religious establishment. The scribes, seeing that Jesus associates with unclean persons, voice their concerns openly but indirectly to Jesus' disciples. Their challenges to Jesus' ministry escalate. Jesus came to call the least, the last, and the lost. In effect, the outsiders are becoming insiders, and the insiders begin to wonder if there is any room left for them.

Today's passage tells us that *anyone* willing to let go of the old self and take on a new identity in Christ is welcome to join the parade. Just know that doing so may ruffle a few feathers.

1. To what extent is your home church willing to get its hands dirty to reach the least, the last, and the lost? Said differently, what are the limits to which your congregation will go to reach a lost person?

2. If a homeless person entered your Sunday morning worship reeking of smoke and body odor, how would your fellow parishioners respond?

3. With whom do you more identify in this episode: Levi or the scribes? Why?

FOUR

Something Old, Something New . . .

Mark 2:18–20 *Now John's disciples and the Pharisees were fasting; and people came and said to him, "Why do John's disciples and the disciples of the Pharisees fast, but your disciples do not fast?"* [19]*And Jesus said to them, "Can the wedding guests fast while the bridegroom is with them? As long as they have the bridegroom* *with them, they cannot fast.* ²⁰*The days will come, when the bridegroom is taken away from them, and then they will fast in that day.*

Understanding the Word. This episode brings to light some currents that have been flowing beneath the surface of the narrative.

No one seemed to object to Jesus' healing on the Sabbath in Capernaum (1:25–26, 31), although it would most certainly have been a violation of the religious laws of that time. Things begin to brew, however, when Jesus proclaims forgiveness over the paralytic. If you will recall, there are scribes on hand. They murmur amongst themselves their concerns about his action, lodging an allegation of blasphemy against him . . . but not so loud as anyone might notice (or so they think). Then, when Jesus sits at the dining table with sinners, those scribes get a bit bolder and ask his disciples (not Jesus himself, mind you) why he eats with them.

Now, in today's account, it is not quite clear who raises the question about fasting. As is sometimes the case in the original language, the Greek is not obvious. However, the context suggests that it is also the scribes who lodge the concern. This time, they go straight to the source and directly confront Jesus about his disciples' practice. This is yet another escalation in the series of controversies involving Jesus' claims of authority.

Jesus responds with a short series of parable-like responses. The first involves a bridegroom and wedding guests. In many instances in the Gospels, Jesus equates himself to a bridegroom in his parables. In the immediately following parables, he employs two parallel word-pictures: one involving cloth and one involving wineskins. In each of these word-pictures, something new is contrasted with something old. And in each, there is a seeming incompatibility between the new and the old. In fact, the new tends to cause a rupture to the old, whether in fabric or wineskin.

In a later week, we'll talk more about the nature of parables, how they function, and why Jesus uses them. For now, we will simply focus on the fact that Jesus represents something new, and the newness creates a threat to the old guard. This is the root of the tension that exists in the Gospels between Jesus and the religious establishment whose understanding of the things of God had become so rigid that there was no room for new understanding. They simply did not have room in their understandings of things to allow for a Messiah like Jesus. It was just too much of a stretch.

In reality, we all wrestle with that to some degree. I know I do. I work hard to come to an understanding of something, and once I've arrived, I get comfortable in that position. I don't want to change. Change is work. Change is uncomfortable. Change *hurts*.

But it seems that pursuing God, at least in this account, requires us to be ever-ready to receive new insights. Not that God is changing, or that truth is transitional. Rather, our limited minds can only absorb so much of an infinite God. *There will never come a day on this earth when we have God entirely figured out.* We will constantly learn. We will constantly grow. We will be *constantly stretched.* Faithful followership demands that we remain a little bit flexible.

1. What issues are currently challenging your congregation to stretch?

2. In many cases, invitations to stretch come from God, who seeks to grant fuller understanding of himself to his people. In other cases, the invitation to stretch comes from the Enemy, who seeks to lead us astray from following God faithfully. Given your congregation's challenges to stretch, which do you think are of God, and which are of the Enemy? How can you distinguish one from the other?

3. How is God currently inviting you to stretch personally in your knowledge and understanding of him?

FIVE

The Letter and the Spirit

Mark 2:23–26 *One sabbath he was going through the grainfields; and as they made their way his disciples began to pluck heads of grain. 24And the Pharisees said to him, "Look, why are they doing what is not lawful on the sabbath?" 25And he said to them, "Have you never read what David did, when he was in need and was hungry, he and those who were with him: 26how he entered the house of God, when Abi´athar was high priest, and ate the bread of the Presence, which it is not lawful for any but the priests to eat, and also gave it to those who were with him?"*

Understanding the Word. In this episode and the one that follows (found in 3:1–5 and discussed on the following page), we read about two controversies regarding the Sabbath. The first involves harvesting, the second involves healing. In both cases, Pharisees challenge Jesus' practices on the Sabbath. In their minds and according to their laws, harvesting and healing constituted work, and were thus violations of the fourth commandment when done on the Sabbath.

Jesus counter-challenges them by questioning their understanding of the law. In so doing, Jesus distinguishes between two aspects of the law: its *letter* and its *spirit*. The letter of the law reads in essence, "do no work." The spirit of the law, however, offers a bigger perspective of God's purposes in creating the command. In fact, the fourth commandment is a bit unique among the Ten Commandments in that it offers a fairly full description of God's intent behind the commandment. Here's the command and its accompanying explanation:

> "Remember the sabbath day, to keep it holy. Six days you shall labor, and do all your work; but the seventh day is a sabbath to the LORD your God; in it you shall not do any work, you, or your son, or your daughter, your manservant, or your maidservant, or your cattle, or the sojourner who is within your gates; for in six days the LORD made heaven and earth, the sea, and all that is in them, and rested the seventh day; therefore the LORD blessed the sabbath day and hallowed it." (Exod. 20:8–11)

Notice two things: (1) this single commandment constitutes about one-third of the words of the whole set of commandments; and (2) the word "for" at the beginning of verse 11 gives us the reason behind the command. It answers the "Why?" question. So in this sense, we have the letter *and* the spirit of the law.

The Pharisees seemed to be overly concerned with the letter of the law to the exclusion of the spirit. In our Scripture reading for today, Jesus' larger concern was that the lives of his disciples be sustained through food, even if that involved a minor infraction of the letter of the law. This really irritated the Pharisees, and when Jesus further humiliated the Pharisees publicly in a confrontation about healing on the Sabbath in Mark 3:1–5, the Pharisees found strange bedfellows with the Herodians, with whom the Pharisees began to conspire to destroy Jesus.

The Pharisees (at least those who were investigating Jesus) did not have the mental flexibility to make room for a fuller understanding of the law. To accept his teaching would bend the Pharisees past their breaking point. Jesus was a threat to them because he challenged their comfort with regard to their beliefs, their identity, and their social status. Jesus declares at the end of this episode that, "The sabbath was made for man, not man for the sabbath; so the Son of man is lord even of the sabbath" (2:27–28). In declaring this, Jesus places himself above both the law and the Pharisees' interpretation of it. This results in a tragic conclusion to this series of confrontations: the religious establishment commits to eliminating the threat of Jesus.

1. What religious rules do you find Christians in your sphere of influence committing to wholeheartedly?

2. Do you observe these Christians pursuing the letter *and* the spirit of the rule? Why or why not?

3. Where in your own life do you observe an overemphasis on the letter of God's law versus its spirit?

4. Let's turn things around for a moment. Is it possible to overemphasize the *spirit* of the law at the expense of its *letter*? If so, how?

COMMENTARY NOTES

General Comments. The scribes are often merely thought of as secretaries. This understanding, however, fails to capture their prominent position in society as experts in matters of religious law. More likely, they probably served a function somewhere between that of our modern-day academic scholars and private legal counsel. The term comes from the Greek word *grammateus* (think, "grammar"), which suggests one who has some knowledge of letters, or a degree of literacy. About a century earlier, a system of stenography ("shorthand") had been developed by the Roman consul Cicero's personal assistant, Tiro. As a result, scribes could record word-for-word accounts of conversations and political proceedings in real time with astonishing accuracy. As agents of the Pharisees (see note 2), the scribes identified in this passage may well have been on hand to document Jesus' activity in the event that charges were brought against him.

General Comments. The Pharisees were a religious sect not entirely unlike a contemporary political party. In a later lesson, we will examine their religious platform. For now, it is only important to note that they were known for their rigorous and exact interpretation of the law. For a Pharisee, maintaining ritual purity through strict observance of the religious law was of utmost concern.

Day 4. Although it is not clear what type of fasting was being practiced here, we know from the Old Testament and passages in the other Gospels that fasting was practiced on a number of occasions and for a variety of reasons. For instance, fasting was commonly associated with grief and mourning (Judges 20:26), guilt and repentance (1 Samuel 7:6), prayerful supplication (2 Samuel 12:16–23), and—on at least one occasion—conspiracy (1 Kings 21:1–14). In the New Testament, fasting can be seen to serve purposes ranging from reliance upon God (Matthew 4:2) to mere ritual observance as a means of attaining righteousness (Luke 18:12). It is not necessary to assume that the fasting observed by John's disciples and the Pharisees was of the same kind.

Day 5. During the time of Jesus, Israel was ruled by a "client king" serving the Roman Empire. The client (or, "puppet") king was appointed by the empire. Jesus was born under Herod the Great (Matthew 2:1), but Herod Antipas was ruling during Jesus' adult years. The Herodians were members of King Herod's court. As royal officials, they most likely would have been seen as individuals who had succumbed to the influence of pagan Hellenism (Greco-Roman cultural influence). As such, the Herodians would have been highly offensive to the Pharisees. That Pharisees sought to conspire with Herodians indicates the degree of hostility and opposition they held against Jesus.

WEEK THREE

GATHERING DISCUSSION OUTLINE

A. Open session in prayer. Ask for specific celebrations of God's goodness.

B. What new insights have you gained from this week's readings? What has encouraged you? What has challenged you?

C. View video for this week's readings.

D. Discuss questions selected from daily readings.

1. **KEY OBSERVATION:** Sometimes our physical structures (church buildings, administrative procedures, church policies) create barriers to outsiders.

   DISCUSSION QUESTION: Where do you see evidence that your church's physical structures (as defined above) unintentionally create barriers to newcomers or outsiders? How do those structures reinforce the distinction between *insiders* and *outsiders*?

2. **KEY OBSERVATION:** Jesus challenged the authority of the insiders by claiming divine authority.

   DISCUSSION QUESTION: Jesus specifically challenged authority in this week's lesson by offering forgiveness of sins to the paralytic. In today's setting, who has the power to forgive sins? Compare various traditions, such as Protestant, Roman Catholic, etc. How does Jesus' divine authority apply to spiritual illness ("sin") *and* physical illness (e.g., paralysis)?

3. **KEY OBSERVATION:** Jesus' invitation to the least, the lost, and the last upset the religious establishment.

   DISCUSSION QUESTION: What issues in your own church seem to be points of conflict between the laity (or members) and the pastoral leadership (or pastor)? As you assess the conflict, which point of view seems to better represent the perspective of Jesus as revealed in Mark 2?

4. **KEY OBSERVATION:** Following Jesus requires us to think outside of our boxes.

   DISCUSSION QUESTION: Two of the most-used statements in churches are "We've never done it that way," and "We've always done it this way." Where do you see evidence of this mentality? How can preserving church traditions be healthy for a kingdom-minded congregation? How can it be damaging?

5. **KEY OBSERVATION:** Jesus was interested in the *spirit* of the law as well as its *letter*.

   DISCUSSION QUESTION: What religious laws do you find easy to follow in letter, but not in spirit? What danger does this pose? How might the *spirit* of the law actually breathe new life into its *letter*? Consider specifically the role of Sabbath in the first two chapters of Mark.

E. What facts and information presented in the commentary portion of the lesson help you understand the weekly Scripture?

F. Close session with prayer. Ask for specific concerns to be brought before our Lord.

WEEK FOUR

Mark 4:1–41

The Parable of the Sower

INTRODUCTION

Typically, we avoid separating verses as we have done here and in the next three lessons. We far prefer to read the text as it is given, verse by verse. However, Mark 4 presents us with a unique circumstance in that Jesus offers a parable (4:2–9), his disciples ask about his use of parables (4:10–13), then Jesus offers an explanation of the parable (4:14–20). What we are doing here is connecting the instruction from the parable with its explanation, giving us more direct access to the point behind each type of soil described. This is in no way intended to be a substitute for a thorough and straightforward reading of the text.

At a surface level, this parable is about agriculture. It illustrates how different seedbeds produce different crops. It also illustrates how the sower is willing to broadcast seed anywhere, *even if the soil doesn't appear to be promising*. But Jesus isn't really interested in farming here, at least not farming for crops. He's more interested in farming for people, in the same way that he called Peter and Andrew to be "fishers of men" in 1:17. One side point that's critical to note here is that God's prevenient grace is evident even here, for *all soils* receive seed.

We, like the disciples with him, are fortunate because Jesus gives us an explanation. But what he doesn't make clear is this: If the seed is the Word, then are the various soil types on which the seed falls stuck in those conditions? Said differently, if the soils represent the types of people who hear the Word, is a person destined to be one and only one type of soil his or her whole life?

As I look at my own life, I see evidence that I am—at different times—typical of each soil type. Some days I'm on fire for the Lord and doing the work of the kingdom with reckless abandon. Other days, I am on fire, but distracted by things that may not be of God. Still other days find me running out of steam quickly because of fatigue. And there are even some days when I simply choose not to listen to the voice of God.

In reality, I flow from one type of soil to another through different seasons of my life, and even through different hours of a day. I think the point here is clearly that God wants us to be the kind of soil that produces a bumper crop. But what if we find ourselves in a spiritual rut, producing nothing, or at best, a crop of thistles?

ONE

Along the Path

Mark 4:3–4, 14–15 *"Listen! A sower went out to sow. ⁴And as he sowed, some seed fell along the path, and the birds came and devoured it. . . .*

¹⁴The sower sows the word. ¹⁵And these are the ones along the path, where the word is sown; when they hear, Satan immediately comes and takes away the word which is sown in them."

Understanding the Word. Jesus places parables before his hearers in part to distinguish the receptive hearers from the unreceptive hearers. Biblical history is full of examples of folks who were unwilling to hear and receive the truth of God. They exhibit a "hardness of heart"; they are "stiff-necked"; they are unwilling to "bend the knee." Moses' encounter with Pharaoh in Exodus is an example. In multiple instances, Scripture reveals that Pharaoh "hardened his heart." For example, "But when Pharaoh saw that there was a respite, he hardened his heart, and would not listen to them; as the LORD had said" (Exod. 8:15). Sometimes God's own people are the unreceptive ones. Also in Exodus, we read: "And [Moses] said, 'If now I have found favor in thy sight, O Lord, let the Lord, I pray thee, go in the midst of us, although it is a stiff-necked people; and pardon our iniquity and our sin, and take us for thy inheritance'" (Exod. 34:9).

The religious leaders of Mark's day are yet another example. As Stephen was about to be stoned to death, he said this about the Jewish leaders: "You stiff-necked people, uncircumcised in heart and ears, you always resist the Holy Spirit. As your fathers did, so do you" (Acts 7:51).

Although these people are described in different ways, their descriptions point to the same reality: in short, they are unwilling to submit to the authority of God.

So how exactly does one become receptive to the Word and will of God? Why does Jesus privilege the Twelve and those with them? We can't be certain, but I suspect it has something to do with the fact that—at least for Peter, Andrew, James, John, and Levi—they were willing to abandon their livelihoods to follow Jesus. They trusted him by stepping out in faith, not knowing what exactly was about to happen next. I think God honored that step in the same way he honored Abraham when God first called Abraham to "Go!" (see Genesis 12:1–3).

God rewards those who genuinely seek him. He exchanges their hard hearts for soft ones: "A new heart I will give you, and a new spirit I will put within you; and I will take out of your flesh the heart of stone and give you a heart of flesh" (Ezek. 36:26).

1. In what areas of life do you sense a hardness toward God's Word and will for your life?

2. Has this hardness always been present, is it fairly recent, or does it come and go?

3. What might be the underlying root of this hardness? How might you remedy this hardness?

TWO

On Rocky Ground

Mark 4:5–6, 16–17 *"Other seed fell on rocky ground, where it had not much soil, and immediately it sprang up, since it had no depth of soil; ⁶and when the sun rose it was scorched, and since it had no root it withered away. . . .*

[16]"And these in like manner are the ones sown upon rocky ground, who, when they hear the word, immediately receive it with joy; [17]and they have no root in themselves, but endure for a while; then, when tribulation or persecution arises on account of the word, immediately they fall away."

Understanding the Word. The chance to receive God's goodness and promise of everlasting life is more than the opportunity of a lifetime. Who in their right mind would not accept such an offer? The problem lies in the fact that such an offer is often put forward by persons who fail to note that grace freely given is not the same as free grace. We will say more about this in a later lesson, but the grace of Jesus is a costly grace . . . costing us everything that stands in the way of true obedience and faithfulness to our Lord.

In Mark chapter 10, a young man approaches Jesus and asks what it would take for him to receive eternal life from Jesus. Jesus responds, "Have you kept all of my commandments?" The man responds, "I have, indeed." Jesus says, "One other thing is required of you: sell all that you have and give to the poor." The man left in sorrow, for he was a rich man (see verses 17–23).

What the man failed to consider in his initial enthusiasm was the true price of following Jesus. Anything that stands in the way of our total submission and complete obedience must be abandoned. Many of us fail to consider the cost of true discipleship, preferring to keep control of certain areas of our lives.

Jesus elsewhere tells us that we should carefully consider the cost of discipleship before eagerly plunging in. On one hand, a man would not consider building a tower without estimating the full cost of the project; otherwise, he would look foolish with an incomplete project as he runs out of funding. Likewise, no military commander goes into battle without first assessing the cost of engaging a particular enemy (see Luke 14:28–33).

A great number of people come to the Lord eagerly and with great enthusiasm when they first hear the message of salvation. Sometimes this is at a revival. Sometimes it's at a crusade, or at a Christian concert, or at a retreat, or on a mission trip. They are excited to accept Jesus as their Savior. However, things get sticky when they realize that such an offer comes with a price tag: Jesus demands our absolute allegiance if he is also to be our Lord. This requires us to abandon all other commitments and to pursue him exclusively. Like the seed that falls on the shallow soil, our eagerness to accept Jesus wilts under the heat and pressure of the true cost of discipleship.

John Wesley is noted for the earth-shaking revival that resulted from his open-air preaching. However, it wasn't just his preaching that stimulated the revival, it was also his commitment to radical discipleship. In his personal journal he writes, "I am more and more convinced, that the devil himself desires nothing more than this, that the people of any place should be half awakened, and then left to themselves to fall asleep again. Therefore I determine, by the grace of God, not to strike one stroke in any place where I cannot follow the blow" (12–13 March 1743).

1. At what points in your life have you received the Word of God with enthusiasm? When was the moment? Where were you, and what were the circumstances?

2. How was the Word presented to you? Were there any costs of discipleship presented along with the offer of God's grace?

3. In what areas of life do you see yourself being surprised by the true costs of discipleship?

THREE

Among Thorns

Mark 4:7, 18–19 *"Other seed fell among thorns and the thorns grew up and choked it, and it yielded no grain. . . .*

¹⁸And others are the ones sown among thorns; they are those who hear the word, ¹⁹but the cares of the world, and the delight in riches, and the desire for other things, enter in and choke the word, and it proves unfruitful."

Understanding the Word. In the second week, we learned that the leper whom Jesus healed disobeyed Jesus by announcing publicly what Jesus had done. This was in strict violation of Jesus' command to the leper to remain silent. The leper had every opportunity to be fruitful in his life as a result of his encounter with Jesus. Instead, he became distracted from the mission on which he was sent. Of course, he may have simply been so overcome with joy that he couldn't stop himself from spreading the word. On the other hand, perhaps it was the temptation of popularity arising from his encounter with

Jesus that distracted him. Or perhaps it was the money he began to earn through speaking engagements. In any case, the growing crowds hindered Jesus' ministry the same way that thorns and thistles hinder the growth of an otherwise fruitful crop.

I know about thistles. Throughout my high school and college years I earned money by working for farmers. One of the main ways I earned that money was also one of the hardest: baling hay (by hand). My wages were a whopping five cents per bale touched. Now, there are two ways to "touch" a bale of hay: one is by stacking the hay bales in the barn. This is like firefighter duty where you have long periods of boredom (as you and the barn crew wait for the next wagon) interrupted only by brief moments of flurry (as everyone scrambles in to get the bales stacked in the stifling, sweltering barn and back out for cool water and fresh air). The other way is to load the wagon in the field behind the tractor and baler. This was typically my job. Unlike barn duty, which tended to be more of a sprinter's game, field duty was a marathon of endurance. Hour after hour, I would steady myself on the slick surface of the wagon, pulling bale after bale after bale off the baler and place it strategically on the wagons so as to tie the entire stack together.

One of the lessons learned in hay baling is how to use your body for leverage so as to exert as little effort moving the bales as possible. The key maneuver in that strategy is to use your knee to provide leverage. As a right-hander, my right knee became my primary point of leverage. I recall one particular day doing some custom hay baling for another farmer. On that day, I literally wore the right knee of my jeans out. This wasn't just because of the constant contact with the scratchy hay, but because the farmer let thistle grow up with his hay. As a result, each bale was worse than sandpaper as it rubbed up against my knee.

Even though the hay crop was successfully bailed and barned, it was seriously compromised by the presence of the thistles. Thorns and thistles compete in the hayfield for the nutrients necessary to the hay's fruitful growth. In the same way, the distractions in our lives rob us of the vital attention we need to be faithful followers of Jesus. The end result is a crop that has failed to reach its potential.

1. What represents the thorns and thistles of your life? In what ways do they distract you?

2. To what degree do these thistles of distraction interfere with or compromise more vital living? How is your walk with Christ impacted? How are your relations with loved ones impacted? How is your work or education impacted?

3. What might you do to begin addressing the problem of thistles in your life?

FOUR

On Good Soil

Mark 4:8, 20 *"And other seeds fell into good soil and brought forth grain, growing up and increasing and yielding thirtyfold and sixtyfold and a hundredfold. . . .*

²⁰But those that were sown upon the good soil are the ones who hear the word and accept it and bear fruit, thirtyfold and sixtyfold and a hundredfold."

Understanding the Word. The goal of the Christian life is to "be fruitful and multiply." This commandment is actually the very first command given to humanity, and it occurs as early as Genesis 1:28. The command is repeated throughout Genesis, including four times during the episode of Noah and the flood, God's do-over. God is interested in fruitful multiplication.

One of the things we notice about the teaching style of Jesus is that he used stories to convey deep truths. The stories typically drew upon the common knowledge of the people of the day. Thus, parables involving planting, cultivating, and harvesting fit well with a culture that was steeped in agriculture. However, the truth of these parables would not be immediately clear to everyone. Instead, they carried with them a sense of mystery. And ironically, it was oftentimes the simpleminded folks who tended to get the point more quickly than the educated.

In this fourth movement of the parable, the story reaches a climax when we learn that some of the seed falls among soil that is hospitable to fruitful growth. And that growth is not only fruitful, it is exponential. It produces a crop vastly larger than what was sown.

Each of these aspects of the parable (the path, the rocky soil, the thistles, and the good soil) is described in various ways throughout Mark's Gospel. In fact, this parable is positioned in the first half of Mark's Gospel as something of a key narration. It underscores and summarizes the nature of people, and the way people respond to the message of Jesus as he proclaims the kingdom of God.

In one sense, fruitful living is fairly obvious. When a Christian shares his or her faith with another Christian, the sharer becomes a sower and the faith is replicated. In some cases, Christians seem to possess extraordinary gifts of evangelism. Billy Graham would certainly seem to be this kind of Christian. But is evangelism the only way we can replicate ourselves by sowing into others? If we look at the teaching of Jesus more carefully, we realize that he came to save people from their circumstances. When we, like Jesus, undertake the task of living Spirit-empowered lives, we become participants in his salvation enterprise. With his power and presence, we sow seeds of justice, mercy, compassion, generosity, faithfulness, and general holiness into the world around us. These seeds are loaded with potential. They, in fact, have the ability to replicate. Christian living might thus be considered a "pay it forward" enterprise. We are *all* called to fruitful living. By our nature, we are created to replicate. That makes each of us a sower. And as Christians, we are called to sow *extravagantly*.

1. We are sometimes hesitant to celebrate the good work that God does in us because it can appear to be bragging. However, acknowledging God's good work in us is always appropriate when we give him the credit. Where do you see God at work in you in ways that are producing fruit?

2. What are the soil conditions of your life that are helping to cultivate a life of fruitful living?

3. How might you encourage others through your own lifestyle and actions to cultivate good soil in their lives?

FIVE

Process vs. Outcome

1 Corinthians 3:4–9 *For when one says, "I belong to Paul," and another, "I belong to Apol'los," are you not merely men? ⁵What then is Apol'los? What is Paul? Servants through whom you believed, as the Lord assigned to each. ⁶I planted, Apol'los watered, but God gave the growth. ⁷So neither he who plants nor he who waters is anything, but only God who gives the growth. ⁸He who plants and he who waters are equal, and each shall receive his wages according to his labor. ⁹For we are God's fellow workers; you are God's field, God's building.*

Understanding the Word. Today's Scripture text is a bit out of order, perhaps, but for good reason.

As a young man born and raised in rural Indiana, I farmed my way through college (as I shared with you earlier this week), and much of what I've learned about life I learned from the man I farmed for. If Tom had an under-producing plot of land on his farm, he wouldn't walk away from it. He would *remediate* it. That means that he would work with it to make it more productive. If the soil was too acidic, he would add lime. If it had too many rocks, he would remove them. If it was hard-packed and crusty, he would till it. If it had weeds, he'd pull them up by the roots. (Actually, he'd send me to do that job.) In short, he would care for that plot until it was able to produce the crop of its potential.

I think this parable is precisely about this point: *remediating* our lives so that we are not only receptive to the Word, but willing to cultivate a climate that is conducive to growth.

I served as a youth pastor for about twelve years prior to pursuing a ministry of teaching at the seminary level. Early in my career, I found myself frustrated because I wasn't seeing the kinds of ministry outcomes for which I had hoped. I was very good at visioning, strategic planning, implementation, and assessment, but what I wasn't good at was achieving results. In short, I could manage the ministry, but I couldn't make it grow.

Then a series of circumstances opened my eyes to a new reality. That reality centered on today's passage from 1 Corinthians in which Paul notes that his role was to plant. Apollos's role was to water. But only God could make the thing grow. I then began to shift my focus from managing *outcome* to managing *process*. I began to be less concerned with my numbers (in terms of event attendance, fundraising dollars, etc.), and more concerned with the way my team and I were going about our ministry efforts. We began to focus more on relationships, and teaching the Word, and God-honoring worship. We believed that our role was simply to set the stage for growth, then trust God with the results.

I cannot tell you how life-giving that awareness was. It was a game changer in terms of my personal ministry, and it has shaped the way I view life. My job is not to manage the outcome or manufacture growth. I am deluded if I believe that. Rather, my job is to cultivate a climate in which growth is likely to happen. That requires me to be diligent in the work that is required of me, and a glimpse of that work is found in the spiritual disciplines practiced by the earliest church: studying the Word, fellowshipping with one another, communing with God and others through worship, and praying (see Acts 2:42–47). John Wesley called these ordinary actions the *means of grace*. These are the activities the church should be engaged in, rather than trying to stimulate numerical growth through gimmicks and campaigns.

If our churches today were more focused on doing the right work (that is, creating climates conducive to growth), I think evangelism would largely be unnecessary. If we were to be the church God has called us to be, I think we would find ourselves in much the same spot Jesus found himself—with people coming down through the roof to be involved. We are not called to be kingdom *growers*. We are called to be climate control technicians, or kingdom *cultivators*.

1. In what ways do you see yourself managing *outcome* instead of *process*? Where in life do you see evidence of this (e.g., coaching, family, work)? How is that working out for you? Does the pursuit of *outcome* lead to satisfying results or a peaceful existence?

2. In what ways might a shift from *outcome* to *process* lead to more fruitful living and more satisfying results? How might such a move open pathways to peace in your life?

3. How might you specifically resolve *today* to invite the Holy Spirit into your efforts so as to "give the growth"?

COMMENTARY NOTES

General Comments. The notion of a seedbed actually gives rise to the notion of the seminary. In Latin, both words come from the same source: *seminarium* (the root *semen* means "seed"). A *seminarium* is a place in which things are cultivated and grown. On a theological campus, minds and hearts are nurtured and grown. In a greenhouse, plants are cultured and grown. Both serve as *seminarii*, or "seminaries." It is therefore no mere coincidence that the publisher of this OneBook Daily-Weekly study on the Gospel of Mark is named Seedbed. This image is as relevant today as it was two thousand years ago as we think about preparing climates that are conducive for making things grow.

Day 1. There is much difficulty in determining whether or not Pharaoh hardened his own heart, or whether God hardened Pharaoh's heart for God's own purposes. Any reading of the narrative in Exodus suggests both likelihoods. For now, we are simply interested in the idea of a heart that resists intrusion or interruption from outside sources.

Day 1. Stephen was a member of a group of seven individuals chosen by the Twelve to assist with the administrative and logistical needs of the early church in Jerusalem. Because of his public profession of Jesus as Christ, he was arrested and tried by the Jewish religious establishment. Upon his conviction, he was sentenced to death by stoning. Just prior to his actual execution, Stephen gives a speech to the religious leaders that culminates in a scathing indictment of the religious establishment. At that point, the rocks begin to fly.

Day 1. The person of Abraham is one of the primary individuals in the history of Israel. Before God called him to leave his home and country and travel to a new land, Abraham's name was simply Abram. During his faithful response to God's call on his life, Abram received a new name from God: Abraham (Gen. 17:5). For simplicity, we will simply refer to him as Abraham throughout the study.

WEEK FOUR

GATHERING DISCUSSION OUTLINE

A. Open session in prayer. Ask for specific celebrations of God's goodness.

B. What new insights have you gained from this week's readings? What has encouraged you? What has challenged you?

C. View video for this week's readings.

D. Discuss questions selected from daily readings.

    1. **KEY OBSERVATION:** In some areas of life, we resist and even reject the Word of God through our hard-heartedness.

    DISCUSSION QUESTION: As a community, how does your church resist the Word of God? What attitudes or commitments do you see at work that consciously resist God's will for your church?

    2. **KEY OBSERVATION:** In other areas of life, we respond to God's Word enthusiastically, only to lose interest at the first signs of difficulty.

    DISCUSSION QUESTION: Think about the ministry efforts of your church, especially those aimed at evangelism. Is the cost of discipleship clearly presented along with the offer of God's grace? How so? Is it possible that knowing the cost of discipleship might actually *increase* people's response to the gospel? (Think about the suspicion someone would have if offered the home of their dreams for one dollar.)

3. **KEY OBSERVATION:** In still other areas of life, we embrace God's Word and nurture it, yet distractions prevent his Word from reaching its full potential.

    DISCUSSION QUESTION: List some of the distractions your church faces. In what ways or areas do various commitments perhaps derail us from God's better purposes? How do things like building maintenance, commitments to excellence, or the pursuit of numerical growth distract us from our primary work?

4. **KEY OBSERVATION:** In some areas of life, however, we embrace and nurture God's Word unto its fullness.

    DISCUSSION QUESTION: Where do you see evidence of fruitful ministry in your local church? Does everyone view this evidence as fruit? Do these efforts receive adequate support from the pulpit and through funding?

5. **KEY OBSERVATION:** All areas of life can be remediated to become fruitful.

    DISCUSSION QUESTION: How should your church balance the needs of start-up enterprises (like new programs and initiatives) while maintaining a commitment to programs that are thriving? What programs may need to be weeded out to make room for new growth?

E. What facts and information presented in the commentary portion of the lesson help you understand the weekly Scripture?

F. Close session with prayer. Ask for specific concerns to be brought before our Lord.

WEEK FIVE

Mark 5:1–6:56

The Matter of Faith

INTRODUCTION

In this week's reading, we will encounter a number of passages in which the faith of persons figures prominently. As we've already seen in several instances, faith requires active, hands-and-feet trust; it is not simply an idea that exists within the safe confines of our minds. But before we begin a discussion of hands-and-feet trust, we need to understand the mind-set behind Jesus' ministry and message.

"In the beginning, God created the heavens and the earth." This is the message of Genesis 1:1. The details of God's creative activity are given throughout the first chapter of Genesis in a day-by-day account. Throughout the course of six days, God speaks the world into existence by his word; he creates domains for things on earth and things in heaven; and on the crowning sixth day of creation, he speaks humanity into creation, declaring all that he had done to be "very good." The earthly home God created for his living creatures was perfect in every possible way. The Hebrew word for this state of perfection is *shalom*, which means something like, "everything is right with the world."

However, as we read beginning in Genesis 3, human rebellion resulted in a fall from the shalom that God intended for humanity. This rebellion was ultimately rooted in self-reliance: a prideful and arrogant pursuit of our own aims instead of God's aims. As a result, humanity descended into a state of brokenness, the outcome of which can only be sin, suffering, and death.

Jesus entered the world knowing both the current state of affairs for humanity and the original shalom God had intended. As God's Son, Jesus set about the work of restoring the world to shalom, and he did that by healing the sick, raising the dead, teaching with authority, and forgiving sinners. As we will see in this week's reading, pride stands at the foundation of the human condition. Jesus provides the solution to that condition. But in order for us to access the solution, we must actively trust Jesus and pursue his aims over our own.

ONE

Seeking Shalom

Mark 5:14–15 *The herdsmen fled, and told it in the city and in the country. And people came to see what it was that had happened. ¹⁵And they came to Jesus, and saw the demoniac sitting there, clothed and in his right mind, the man who had had the legion; and they were afraid.*

Understanding the Word. Two things about today's reading are noteworthy. First, the demoniac is found to be "clothed and in his right mind" (v. 15). This points to the fact that the man has found shalom. The second point, however, is a bit surprising: when the people from the city and the country show up to see what happened, Mark reports that "they were afraid" (v. 15). Why would people fear shalom?

In a very real way, this episode serves as an example of both Jesus' mission and an appropriate human response to that mission. However, as we will see over the next few days, not all responses to Jesus' mission and work are so appropriate. In fact, this scene of the demoniac hints at the problem when Mark reports that some people, upon finding the demoniac clothed and in his right mind, were afraid. Fear can thus be seen as a driving force in opposition to shalom.

But how does fear oppose shalom? I must first say that it is not fear alone that is the problem. In reality, fear is merely a symptom of a deeper "dis-ease." Fear is the fruit of pride. It is a consequence of recognizing the inadequacy of our own attempts at self-reliance. Pride exerts itself in multiple ways, but two of the most common of those ways are *anger* and *shame*. *Anger* results when the world around us does not live into our prideful expectations. *Shame* results when we do not live into the world's prideful expectations.

In both cases, we abandon God's expectations either by *creating* false ones (which others cannot and perhaps should not try to live into) or by *accepting* false ones (which we allow others to place upon us).

Notice how the demoniac simply submits to the authority of Jesus. There are no ifs, ands, or buts. However, as we will see later this week, pride (in various forms) stands in the way of Jesus' willingness to bring shalom to a broken world. Fundamentally, there are two authorities in competition with one another: the authority of God and the authority of humanity. When the authority of God is replaced by the authority of humanity, shalom is no longer accessible, brokenness becomes more prevalent, and we respond in fear that: (1) the world will not live into our expectations, and (2) we will not live into the world's expectations. Why does Mark report that some were afraid when they found the demoniac clothed and in his right mind? Although we can't be certain, it seems likely (based on the passages to follow) that Jesus did not operate within the people's tried-and-true expectations, and as a result, his ministry was a threat to their understanding of the world.

1. In what areas of life do you experience anger because people around you do not live into your expectations of them?

2. In what areas of life do you experience shame because you do not live into expectations people around you have of you?

3. How are your expectations of others and the expectations others have of you grounded in biblical truth? How might they be unbiblical?

TWO

The Power of Testimony

Mark 5:18–20 *And as [Jesus] was getting into the boat, the man who had been possessed with demons begged him that he might be with him.* [19]*But he refused, and said to him, "Go home to your friends, and tell them how much the Lord has done for you, and how he has had mercy on you."* [20]*And he went away and began to proclaim in the Decapolis how much Jesus had done for him; and all men marveled.*

Understanding the Word. Today's passage serves as a fitting closure to the scene that began in verse 2. There, we find Jesus getting out of a boat. Once on land, he heals a demoniac. But before the scene with the demoniac closes, Mark gives us a literary clue that the resolution to the scene is before us: Jesus gets back into the boat (v. 18).

You will note how in this story Jesus accomplished exactly what he set out to do, which was to bring shalom. Perhaps more important, all men marveled (v. 20). This closing bracket to Mark's longest healing story brings this episode to an appropriate conclusion. Although the story seemed to initially conclude in a moment of fear (v. 15), the scene actually climaxes on a more positive note: "all men marveled" (v. 20). What explains the shift from fear to marvel? One possible (and perhaps likely) explanation is the power of the former demoniac's testimony. Note that Jesus sent the man back to his home to report all that had happened to him. Note also that Jesus' command to the man to return to his village was counter to what the man wanted (to travel with Jesus as a disciple). So why wouldn't Jesus have simply enlisted the man in Jesus' growing number of traveling disciples?

Over my years of thinking about God's call on my life and on the lives of others, it occurs to me that not everyone receives the same calling. Not everyone is expected to respond to Jesus the same way. Certainly, some are called to leave families, homes, and jobs to pursue his calling. But as I read this passage today, it occurs to me that sometimes we are called to be in ministry at home.

The man formerly possessed by a legion of demons was so overwhelmed with gratitude that he wanted to accompany Jesus. In fact, he *begged* Jesus to let him go with him. He was willing to leave everything (which, for him, wasn't much there among the tombs and such), but Jesus sent him home to testify to his community about the amazing work Jesus had done in the man's life.

And the man obeyed.

This stands in tension, perhaps, with the account of the leper healed in chapter 1. Jesus commanded him to remain silent. That was Jesus' plan. Here, though, Jesus sends the former demoniac home to publicly share his story. Whereas the leper disobeyed with the result that Jesus' ministry was impeded, the demoniac's obedience created marvel among the townspeople.

What if the demoniac had disobeyed? What if he told Jesus that he would return to his home, but instead he followed Jesus at a distance? What would the consequences have been? Imagine how much blander life in the Decapolis would have been had they not received the reports of Jesus and his saving powers. The demoniac *trusted* Jesus, even when doing so conflicted with the man's deepest desire. And the good news of Jesus spread, replacing fear with marvel.

1. Why might the people from the city and the country initially have been fearful when they saw the demoniac clothed and in his right mind?

2. How might the demoniac's personal testimony have helped them turn their fear into marvel?

3. What part of your own journey in faith might be a source of encouragement to others? Said differently, where do you have opportunities to tell your story to others in ways that help them overcome their fear of religion, faith, or commitment to the church?

THREE

Faith and Fear

Mark 5:21–24, 35–36 *And when Jesus had crossed again in the boat to the other side, a great crowd gathered about him; and he was beside the sea. ²²Then came one of the rulers of the synagogue, Ja'irus by name; and seeing him, he fell at his feet, ²³and besought him, saying, "My little daughter is at the point of death. Come and lay your hands on her, so that she may be made well, and live." ²⁴And he went with him.*

And a great crowd followed him and thronged about him. . . .

³⁵While he was still speaking, there came from the ruler's house some who said, "Your daughter is dead. Why trouble the Teacher any further?" ³⁶But ignoring what they said, Jesus said to the ruler of the synagogue, "Do not fear, only believe."

Understanding the Word. As a ruler of the local synagogue, Jairus is in some way part of the religious establishment. It is important to note here that Mark is relating real persons and real events. In fiction, authors sometimes tend to make members of a group all the same. If Mark's Gospel were fiction, *all* members of the establishment would probably oppose Jesus.

But that's not how life typically works in reality. For example, not all Republicans feel the same way about gun control. Not all Democrats think the same way about health care reform. Not all United Methodists agree on worship music, and not all persons in central Kentucky root for UK basketball. (Well, on that one, I might be wrong.) My point is this: in reality, life is more complex than stereotypes that pigeonhole a member of a group into one and only one way of thinking. Jairus is just such an example.

Anyone who has lost a child knows grief in ways that the rest of us probably (and hopefully) will never know. Jairus is *desperate*. He—a leader of his people—falls at the feet of Jesus in complete surrender. He is willing to do anything to save his daughter. His last recourse is a bold one: to seek out the One whom the religious leaders had conspired to destroy. In so doing, Jairus chooses a side.

It's interesting that the voices of human reason around Jairus try to convince him that all hope is lost, and that he should simply accept the outcome. There is no room for a miracle, and no expectation for one. Jesus apparently feels a bit differently.

It's also interesting that Jesus commands Jairus not to fear, but to believe (v. 36). Those around Jairus, however, are causing him to waiver in his confidence. Jesus seeks to steady Jairus's resolve. As we saw in the first week's lesson, to *believe* means more than merely accepting something as true or factual. It means to trust. In the face of the pressure of his peers, Jairus risks looking like an absolute idiot by continuing with his plea in the face of an unchangeable circumstance. Jesus counters that pressure by urging Jairus not to fear. I think it's worth noting here that the opposite of belief in this instance is not doubt, but fear. This makes perfect sense when we understand "to believe" as "to trust" rather than merely "to think."

1. Why do you think Mark mentions that Jairus, when he saw Jesus, fell at Jesus' feet? What's the significance of this detail?

2. Jairus was willing to abandon his daughter in her dying moment to seek help. What does this suggest about his level of desperation?

3. In your mind, what is the opposite of faith? Does it surprise you that Jesus would point to fear as the opposite of faith? How is fear related to faith?

4. What did Jairus fear that kept him from full faith? What do you fear that keeps you from full faith?

FOUR

Shalom and Shame

Mark 5:24–29 *And [Jesus] went with [Ja′irus].*

And a great crowd followed him and thronged about him. ²⁵And there was a woman who had had a flow of blood for twelve years, ²⁶and who had suffered much under many physicians, and had spent all that she had, and was no better but rather grew worse. ²⁷She had heard the reports about Jesus, and came up behind him in the crowd and touched his garment. ²⁸For she said, "If I touch even his garments, I shall be made well." ²⁹And immediately the hemorrhage ceased; and she felt in her body that she was healed of her disease.

Understanding the Word. This account of the woman with the uncontrollable hemorrhage is nested between segments of the account of the healing of Jairus's daughter. In literary terms, it is *intercalated*, meaning placed between two parts of a larger scene. The reason it is there is probably because that's how the events unfolded. Sometimes in life things happen that way.

The woman had exhausted her options. Doctors could no longer help her. In fact, they were making her condition worse. As a woman with a blood issue, she was ritually unclean, meaning she could have no contact with others (see Leviticus 15:25–27 for the statement of this law). She was living a "less than" existence.

Mark 1:24 introduces the scene by stating that a great crowd was following Jesus, even thronging about him. That makes for some pretty close quarters.

The fact that the woman made her way to Jesus indicates that she likely did some pushing and shoving to get there. In so doing, she would have "contaminated" each person she touched. Those folks would not have appreciated it . . .

at all. It may have even earned her a death sentence, depending on how local readings of the law were made.

Likewise, the fact that she came up behind Jesus indicates that she wasn't seeking permission. She wanted to stay out of view. She probably thought of herself as a thief stealing a cure from Jesus' garment. She was a pretty desperate woman making a pretty risky move. It was an all-or-nothing effort.

> And Jesus, perceiving in himself that power had gone forth from him, immediately turned about in the crowd, and said, "Who touched my garments?" And his disciples said to him, "You see the crowd pressing around you, and yet you say, 'Who touched me?'" And he looked around to see who had done it. But the woman, knowing what had been done to her, came in fear and trembling and fell down before him, and told him the whole truth. (Mark 5:30–33)

Imagine her initial and overwhelming delight when she sensed her immediate healing. Also imagine her overwhelming and sudden terror when Jesus turned and demanded, "Who touched me?"

BUSTED—or so she thought.

"And he said to her, 'Daughter, your faith has made you well; go in peace, and be healed of your disease'" (Mark 5:34).

In a moment of repentance (or defeat), the woman confessed. She admitted her guilt, fell at his feet in a posture of humility, and told him the entire truth. Now imagine her astonishment when Jesus dismissed her without punishment. In fact, he dismissed her with a blessing to go in peace.

The woman's thoughts about Jesus didn't heal her. Her doctrine didn't save her. Her theology didn't rescue her. Her *faith* saved her. Here, "faith" (*pistis*) is closely related to "to believe" (*pisteuō*). It was her *trust* in Jesus' power that saved her, and her trust was confirmed by the risk she took to access his power.

1. How does this two-part phrase impact your reading of the woman's circumstance: she "had spent all that she had, and was no better but rather grew worse"?

2. How might shame have been an obstacle to her healing? How might shame be an obstacle to your own healing?

3. What does Jesus mean when he says "go in peace" (think, shalom)? What does shalom look like for you?

FIVE

Prophets without Honor

Mark 6:10–13 *And [Jesus] said to [his disciples], "Where you enter a house, stay there until you leave the place. ¹¹And if any place will not receive you and they refuse to hear you, when you leave, shake off the dust that is on your feet for a testimony against them." ¹²So they went out and preached that men should repent. ¹³And they cast out many demons, and anointed with oil many that were sick and healed them.*

Understanding the Word. I cannot, for the life of me, understand why someone would not embrace a life in the gospel, or would fail to accept Jesus' promise of new life. I just don't get it.

I suppose in many cases, folks reject what they're presented with, and what they're presented with may be a false representation of Jesus and his gospel. That makes sense. As I thumb through cable channels I see lots of brands of Christianity that frankly aren't very attractive, even to me. They are either too syrupy (with everything sugar-coated and no engagement with the real world) or they are too focused on health-and-wealth ("Just send in your gift and you will be *blessed!*").

On the heels of Jesus' healing of Jairus's daughter and the woman with the bleeding disorder, Jesus returns to his hometown. Ironically, Jesus is met with suspicion and doubt instead of worship and celebration. In a surprising twist of events, the people who knew Jesus best were the ones who most failed to recognize his true authority.

As I shared before, sometimes people misrepresent the gospel. But when Jesus sent out his disciples two-by-two, I think those disciples presented the gospel and Jesus accurately. Some simply would not receive the message. Perhaps in some cases it was because they were closet devil-worshippers (although I doubt it). I think more likely folks were too comfortable in their modes of living, unwilling to risk a change.

I grew up with a saying: an old dog will lie on a porch nail until it becomes too painful to do so any longer.

People are like that. *I'm* sometimes like that. There are occasions when we settle for an existence that is in so many ways less than God intended for us.

For some, merely living without pain or crisis is the highest aim, yet there may be no joy in living. It's easier to stay behind locked doors than to venture out to experience the world. For others, getting off the couch to exercise is simply too much work, even though they despise their obesity. For others, staying in destructive relationships is preferable to being alone. In all instances, people are settling for less.

I suppose that some of those doors the early disciples knocked on belonged to people like these. I don't think they were evil people necessarily. I think they were afraid—afraid of change, afraid of something different. And it was their fear that prevented them from receiving the good news about Jesus. As a result, he told the disciples simply to move on with their message.

Again, we see that the gospel awaits an invitation. It tends not to impose itself on others. You've perhaps seen the painting of Jesus standing outside a door, knocking. One interesting thing about the painting is this: there is no doorknob on the outside face of the door; it can only be opened from the inside.

Some indeed refuse to open their doors to Jesus. But for those who *are* willing, Jesus promises to remain with them: "Behold, I stand at the door and knock; if any one hears my voice and opens the door, I will come in to him and eat with him, and he with me" (Rev. 3:20).

1. Why do you suppose Jesus' family and hometown friends would struggle to accept his authority and status as the Son of God?

2. How is the phrase "shake off the dust that is on your feet" significant? What might that have meant back then? What might it mean today?

3. What are your ministry and witness like at home? How do your family members and closest friends accept your testimony and lifestyle as a follower of Jesus? What aspects of your life and witness give others reason to be suspicious of your testimony?

COMMENTARY NOTES

General Comments. The Greek word for "word" is *logos*. The apostle John begins his Gospel with a prologue that describes the role of the logos in creation. Central to the description that John provides are three main points. First, the logos exists eternally: "In the beginning was the Word [logos], and the Word was with God, and the Word was God" (John 1:1). Second, the logos was instrumental in God's act of creation: "all things were made through him [referring to the logos], and without him was not anything made that was made" (John 1:3). Third, the logos became human in the form of Jesus: "And the Word [logos] became flesh and dwelt among us, full of grace and truth; we have beheld his glory, glory as of the only Son from the Father" (John 1:14). With this in mind, we can begin to see how salvation history reaches from creation (in Genesis) to new creation (in Revelation). It is a primary concern for Mark to locate Jesus as God-incarnate (God "in the flesh") within the context of salvation history. In so doing, Mark reveals Jesus' central mission: to restore a broken world to the shape it was originally designed to maintain. Prior to Adam's and Eve's fall into sin, they enjoyed untarnished existence. Jesus came to usher in a new era in which the kingdom of God would take root in the minds and hearts of people. He also came to overcome the effects of sin and death on the physical world. As a result, healing was a major part of his ministry.

Day 2. The name *Decapolis* is a combination of two Greek word roots: "deca" (meaning "ten"; think "decade" or "decathalon") and "polis" (meaning "city"; think "Indianapolis"). *Decapolis* was a group of ten cities that perhaps participated in some sort of federation or league of cities, as they shared a number of things in common with respect to culture, language, economy, etc.

WEEK FIVE

GATHERING DISCUSSION OUTLINE

A. Open session in prayer. Ask for specific celebrations of God's goodness.

B. What new insights have you gained from this week's reading? What has encouraged you? What has challenged you?

C. View video for this week's readings.

D. Discuss questions selected from daily readings.

    1. **KEY OBSERVATION:** Fear opposes shalom and is rooted in pride.

    DISCUSSION QUESTION: In light of this key observation, what relationship does pride have to shalom? What is the basis of pride? What is the basis of shalom?

    2. **KEY OBSERVATION:** Personal testimony can turn the volume down on fear.

    DISCUSSION QUESTION: Suppose you felt the Lord leading you to do something crazy with your life, like sell all your possessions and move to the jungles of South America as a missionary. How fearful would you be? Suppose also that a missionary from South America comes to your church and shares her testimony about her time there. How might that impact your fear?

    3. **KEY OBSERVATION:** Faith is the remedy for fear.

DISCUSSION QUESTION: In what areas of life do you find it especially difficult to trust ("have faith in") Jesus? How does fear prevent you from experiencing a fuller measure of God's reliability?

4. **KEY OBSERVATION:** Shame can be a form of pride that stands in the way of shalom.

   DISCUSSION QUESTION: Discuss the ways shame keeps people in your life from experiencing peace. How might shame also be keeping *you* from experiencing peace?

5. **KEY OBSERVATION:** Living faithfully at home can be an enormous challenge.

   DISCUSSION QUESTION: As you reflect on your Christian witness among those closest to you (best friends, immediate family members, roommates, etc.), how would they describe your witness? Does your witness help others to overcome their fear of trusting God, or does it actually increase their anxieties about trusting him? How so?

E. What facts and information presented in the commentary portion of the lesson help you understand the weekly Scripture?

F. Close session with prayer. Ask for specific concerns to be brought before our Lord.

WEEK SIX

Mark 7:1–8:26

Inside-Out Faith

INTRODUCTION

Some time back, several church staff members and I attended a large church conference. One of the speakers was talking about traditions and practices we observe in our churches today, but without any real reason. He shared a story about a visit he had once made to a small congregation.

At one point in the service, all of the congregants stood up, turned to the back of the sanctuary, and together recited the Apostle's Creed. Then they turned back around, sat down, and resumed their order of worship. The conference speaker later asked one of the members of the church why they turned and faced the back of the church. The member paused, and finally answered, "I'm not really sure. We've just always done it that way . . . at least as long as I can remember."

The speaker became curious about the matter, and did a little investigating. He later learned that years prior, before church bulletins were printed and distributed to the congregation, the congregation would recite the Apostle's Creed by reading it from a large plaque mounted to the wall. The plaque was at the back of the church, so all the congregants would turn to face it, read it, then turn back to the front.

At the time of the conference speaker's visit to the church, everyone had printed bulletins that included the Apostle's Creed neatly printed in it. Further, the plaque on the back wall had long since be removed. They held to the practice, but for no real reason.

I wonder if any of our own practices lack real reason. Or perhaps there's a reason we do what we do, but we are just unaware of that reason. This week's lessons will largely deal with external, or outer, practices . . . what John Wesley described as "having the form of religion without the power" (Thoughts Upon Methodism, 1786). How many things do we do in worship, in ministry, or in everyday life on behalf of Christ and his kingdom that have no real reason? Worse yet, how many of those things do we maintain in hopes of being good Christians?

ONE

The Traditions of the Elders

Mark 7:5–8 *And the Pharisees and the scribes asked him, "Why do your disciples not live according to the tradition of the elders, but eat with hands defiled?"* *⁶And he said to them, "Well did Isaiah prophesy of you hypocrites, as it is written, 'This people honors me with their lips, but their heart is far from me; ⁷in vain do they worship me, teaching as doctrines the precepts of men.' ⁸You leave the commandment of God, and hold fast the tradition of men."*

Understanding the Word. We have things a bit out of order in this lesson. We should really begin with verses 1–4, which include a discussion about the Pharisees. However, one can't really relate to the Pharisees without understanding what the traditions of the elders are. So, let's do a bit of a history lesson.

The traditions (*paradosin*, or "things handed on") of the elders were a set of oral laws developed to accompany the written law of the Old Testament (the *Torah*, which means either "law" or "instruction"). Those oral laws have their origins in the period when the Jews were allowed to return to Jerusalem following their captivity in Babylon in the sixth century BC.

Jerusalem had been sacked by the Babylonians. The temple had been destroyed. And the best and brightest of the Israelites had been exiled to Babylon where they were held captive for about seventy years. (This is a bit of a review from Week 1.) Israel's crime had been apostasy, meaning that God's people had pursued foreign gods in direct violation of the first commandment. They understood their time of exile to be a period of punishment.

Upon their return to Jerusalem, the Jews vowed to never let such apostasy happen again. So, in order to ensure that none of the provisions of Torah were violated, they developed a set of oral instructions designed to buffer the written law. In effect, the oral law became a hedge of protection for the written law. Here is the rationale: if one does not violate the oral law, then there is no possibility of violating the written law.

I actually find myself at times developing my own oral laws at my house. For instance, I'll pour myself a refreshing beverage (Pepsi-Cola in a twelve-ounce glass bottle is my drink of choice, but they're hard to find these days), and instantly four little faces are at my side, wanting a drink. Because I have a highly developed sense of property rights, I say, "No!" but in a kind, Jesus-loving way. If I have to get up to answer the phone, I say very clearly to my boys, "Don't touch my refreshing beverage. *Don't even LOOK at it!*" And thus, with the additional statement, I've created an oral law—a hedge of protection around the first.

The oral laws, or traditions of the elders, became increasingly complex over time. Only the religious scholars (the scribes) were capable of interpreting and enforcing them. By the time of Jesus, they had really outgrown their usefulness, and instead became an artificial system of religious dos and don'ts that maintained little relevance to the spirit behind the original Torah. These are the traditions that the Pharisees particularly prided themselves in upholding. And these are the traditions that Jesus challenged as mere "precepts of men" (v. 7).

1. Where do you see evidence today that Christians might be expecting *less* of Christians than God expects of Christians?

2. Where do you see evidence today that Christians might be expecting *more* of Christians than God expects of Christians?

3. What are the possible benefits of each circumstance? What are the possible dangers?

TWO

Meet the Pharisees

Mark 7:1–4 *Now when the Pharisees gathered together to him, with some of the scribes, who had come from Jerusalem, ²they saw that some of his disciples ate with hands defiled, that is, unwashed. ³(For the Pharisees, and all the Jews,*

do not eat unless they wash their hands, observing the tradition of the elders;
⁴and when they come from the market place, they do not eat unless they purify
themselves; and there are many other traditions which they observe, the washing
of cups and pots and vessels of bronze.)

Understanding the Word. The sect of the Pharisees was a little bit like a
blend of a political party and a religious denomination. They held to a set of
beliefs and practices that set them apart from other Jewish sects. (We'll take a
closer look at some of those sects in Week 9.) The Pharisees had their origins in
the time when the Jews were returning to Jerusalem from Babylon (mentioned
in yesterday's lesson). They came to be strict interpreters of the law, and strict
practitioners, as well.

Today, we often think of Pharisees as hypocrites. Although there is reason
for thinking in this way, it really is something of an overgeneralization. Not
all Pharisees were hypocrites, or perhaps better said, not all Pharisees were
entirely hypocritical. To be a Pharisee was to love and honor God through a
very strict obedience to the law. Over the centuries, the Pharisees organized
largely to separate themselves from those Jewish elements that were embracing
pagan, Greek practices.

A first-century Jewish historian named Josephus provides us with the
most detailed information about the Pharisees. He tells us that the Pharisees
believed in the resurrection of the body, in eternal punishment and reward,
in a balance of human free will and divine determinism, and in following the
oral law (as we've already noted). These and other elements help define the
Pharisaic party.

In today's passage, we get a glimpse into the life of the Pharisees through
something of a sidebar comment by Mark. Verses 3–4 are in parentheses, but
this is a modern convention. The original Greek text written by Mark would
have consisted entirely of upper-case letters, with no spaces between words,
and no punctuation marks. One reason for thinking that we should treat these
two verses as parenthetical is because we could actually read from verse 2
straight to verse 5, skipping verses 3–4, and the text would flow perfectly. Here
is how it would read without verses 3–4:

Now when the Pharisees gathered together to him, with some of the scribes,
who had come from Jerusalem, they saw that some of his disciples ate with

hands defiled, that is, unwashed. . . . And the Pharisees and the scribes asked him, "Why do your disciples not live according to the tradition of the elders, but eat with hands defiled?"

Even though Mark did not have parentheses marks available to him, he could still insert a parenthetical thought, and I suspect that he has done so here because he expects at least some of his readers to be unfamiliar with these customs. This helps us define—in part—his audience, and may represent one of his reading cues: Mark is writing to an audience wider than Judaism.

1. Why is it important to consider that Mark might be writing to an audience wider than Judaism?

2. Mark takes the time to explain these traditions so the reader can understand. What does this suggest about Mark's strategy or intent as a Gospel writer?

3. How might such rigorous obedience to the law serve to honor God? How might it dishonor him?

THREE

Inner Religion

Mark 7:9–15 *And he said to them, "You have a fine way of rejecting the commandment of God, in order to keep your tradition!* [10]*For Moses said, 'Honor your father and your mother'; and, 'He who speaks evil of father or mother, let him surely die';* [11]*but you say, 'If a man tells his father or his mother, What you would have gained from me is Corban' (that is, given to God)—*[12]*then you no longer permit him to do anything for his father or mother,* [13]*thus making void the word of God through your tradition which you hand on. And many such things you do."*

[14]*And he called the people to him again, and said to them, "Hear me, all of you, and understand:* [15]*there is nothing outside a man which by going into him can defile him; but the things which come out of a man are what defile him."*

Understanding the Word. The reason the Pharisees take so much heat from Jesus in his day and from us in our day is really twofold. First, they focus too much on external faith. That is, they concern themselves with outer religion . . . what to do and not do, what to eat and not eat, where to go and not go . . . etc. These are all things that are visible on the outside. Second, they—in some cases—fail to practice what they preach. This is what earns them the name "hypocrite," for they merely play-act at being faithful followers of God, setting one standard for those around them, but creating exceptions for themselves.

However, a closer look at the Pharisees may give us some insights that are a bit more balanced.

At the time of Mark's writing, Judaism had fractured into a number of sects, or factions. Again, we'll discuss these in more detail in Week 9, but for now we can say this. Greco-Roman culture had spread across the Holy Land in ways that were a mixed bag. On one hand, there were some real benefits: roads were built and educational systems were put into place. On the other, Greco-Roman paganism crept in at every point. Jewish responses to Hellenism (the expansion of Greek culture) varied. Some embraced it, thinking it was a great opportunity for the Jews to be a part of a progressive movement. Others opposed it to the point of military resistance. Still others simply withdrew to the desert and lived in isolated compounds.

Some, however, sought to remain faithful to God *and* persist in the face of the advances of Hellenism. You might say that these were the ones who chose to be "in the world, but not of it." As you can likely imagine, this was a tough position, for it required those Jews to maintain a delicate balancing act between standing apart and blending in. The Pharisees chose that position, and it was a difficult one, indeed. They pursued holiness, and sought to inform and influence the rural commoners (the "people of the land") to likewise pursue holiness.

In so many ways, John Wesley's program of evangelism and discipleship in eighteenth-century England was very much like the original intent of the Pharisees. He took his ministry to the streets. He used his Oxford training to bring biblical literacy to the common people. He demonstrated a genuine concern for the physical health of persons as well as their spiritual health. He advocated holiness, offering people a glimpse of new life through joyful obedience.

The Pharisees, at least some of them, drifted over time in terms of their orientation. No longer did they concern themselves with the *spirit* of God's law; instead, they began to focus entirely on the *letter*. As a result, they lost sight of the reason God's law existed in the first place. Theirs was an outer religion. Jesus' challenge to them pertained to the inward condition of their hearts and minds. John Wesley shared the same concern. I wonder if we should likewise.

1. Think back to the lesson in this week's introduction about the Apostle's Creed. Where do you see instances of your church clinging to practices that don't seem to have any real meaning?

2. As you reflect on these practices, would it be best if the church simply abandoned these practices? If so, why? If not, why not?

3. Think about your own moral code. What personal morals do you maintain simply because you think doing so is the right thing to do? Can you identify a *spirit* behind the *letter* of that part of your moral code?

FOUR

Going Viral

Mark 8:15–18 *And he cautioned them, saying, "Take heed, beware of the leaven of the Pharisees and the leaven of Herod." ¹⁶And they discussed it with one another, saying, "We have no bread." ¹⁷And being aware of it, Jesus said to them, "Why do you discuss the fact that you have no bread? Do you not yet perceive or understand? Are your hearts hardened? ¹⁸Having eyes do you not see, and having ears do you not hear? And do you not remember?"*

Understanding the Word. The setting for this scene, like so many in Mark, is the Sea of Galilee. Jesus had just fed a crowd of several thousand with seven loaves of bread and a few small fish. Not only was everyone satisfied, but there were seven baskets of leftovers.

This wasn't the first time Jesus had fed so many with so little. In chapter 6, Jesus fed another, even larger crowd with five loaves and two fish. On that occasion, there were twelve baskets of leftovers (vv. 37–44).

The occasion for Jesus' word of warning regarding the leaven (or yeast) of the Pharisees happens after the second feeding of the multitude. On the heels of that spectacular event, the Pharisees demand a sign from Jesus . . . right after he had just fed thousands with a single bag of groceries.

Curious.

Jesus then makes a comparison between himself and the Pharisees. Steeped in the traditions of the elders, the Pharisees seek to make converts. Matthew's Gospel records it this way: "Woe to you, scribes and Pharisees, hypocrites! for you traverse sea and land to make a single proselyte [or "convert"], and when he becomes a proselyte, you make him twice as much a child of hell as yourselves" (Matt. 23:15).

They do, in fact, honor the second part of the original commandment to creation we discussed in Week 4: to multiply. The problem is this: their fruit is rotten. They are replicating error, and on a massive scale. In the same way that just a little bit of yeast leavens the entire lump of dough, so too does the teaching of the scribes and Pharisees impact the whole of Judaism. It is like a virus that has mutated and begins replicating itself uncontrollably. (Like a good YouTube video, it "goes viral.")

Jesus' teaching and ministry likewise go viral. We see evidence of that in the way the crowd grows quickly to become throngs of people, and how the surrounding areas begin passing on his message and reports of his mighty works.

In a classic Christian work entitled *Mere Christianity*, C. S. Lewis (the author of *The Chronicles of Narnia*) describes the spread of genuine Christian faith as a "good infection." This is a terrific image. We see the effect when Jesus feeds the multitudes with a minimal amount of food. He takes the fruit of the field (wheat grain) and the fruit of the sea (fish), and multiplies them in ways that demonstrate fulfillment of the first commandment to creation.

When Jesus asks the disciples on the boat why they are worried about not having bread, he challenges them. Those with Jesus discovered that they had only one loaf. Boats weren't big back then, at least not by modern standards. They were probably in a fishing boat that perhaps at most could have carried a dozen people. Remembering the multitudes that had just been fed, those with Jesus should have figured out that dividing one loaf among twelve or so guys—using Jesus' math—would have ensured that all would be filled to the gills. But they were afraid they would not have enough. They were going to go hungry. The idea went viral.

Jesus was quick to provide the appropriate vaccine for the virus . . .

"When I broke the five loaves for the five thousand, how many baskets full of broken pieces did you take up?" They said to him, "Twelve." "And the seven for the four thousand, how many baskets full of broken pieces did you take up?" And they said to him, "Seven." And he said to them, "Do you not yet understand?" (Mark 8:19–21)

1. Notice how today's passage demonstrates that Jesus' disciples worried that they would not have enough food to eat. How does Jesus' response in 8:19–21 relate to the leaven that Jesus talks about in 8:15? Note especially Jesus' rebuke in 8:17–18.

2. In both Scripture and the world today, what kinds of attitudes can be represented by leaven?

3. How does this discussion of the leaven of the Pharisees speak to issues of faith and fear?

4. Where do you see evidence in your own life of leaven at work?

FIVE

Witness Protection Program

Mark 8:22–26 *And they came to Beth-sa'ida. And some people brought to him a blind man, and begged him to touch him. ²³And he took the blind man by the hand, and led him out of the village; and when he had spit on his eyes and laid his hands upon him, he asked him, "Do you see anything?" ²⁴And he looked up and said, "I see men; but they look like trees, walking." ²⁵Then again he laid his hands upon his eyes; and he looked intently and was restored, and saw everything clearly. ²⁶And he sent him away to his home, saying, "Do not even enter the village."*

Understanding the Word. At moments, Scripture can be a bit comical. I'm thinking at the moment of Jesus' exasperation with the Pharisees in yesterday's lesson. Recall that he had just fed thousands with a few loaves of bread and small fish. In 8:11 the Pharisees begin to argue with him (presumably about his authority and what gives him the right to do such-and-such), asking for a sign from him to test him.

At this point, Jesus can only shrug his shoulders and sigh. I envision him tilting his head back, closing his eyes, and exhaling very, very deeply: "*Idiots!*"

Not many scenes are comical, and the passage for today's reading is definitely not one of them. It's easy to get hung up on the fact that Jesus heals the man's vision in two takes. What strikes me, however, is the fact that Jesus does not send the man into the city to proclaim the mighty work done in his life. Jesus doesn't send the man to the priest to make the appropriate offering. He sends him home. *Straight* home. The translation above highlights the Greek intensifying word *mēde*, meaning "not even."

We've encountered this word before in Mark, we just may not have noticed. In 2:2, Mark tells us that the four men lower the paralytic through the roof because there was no room in the house, *not even* at the door. In 3:20, the crowds in the house were so thick that Jesus and his disciples could *not even* eat. I shared my own use of a *mēde* phrase earlier this week when I shared with you that I forbid my boys to drink my refreshing beverage. In fact, I charge them to *not even* look at it.

Jesus commands the man to go home, to *not even* enter the village. Why? Although we cannot know for sure, I suspect it's because the Pharisees and scribes were ramping up their opposition to Jesus and beginning to look for an opportunity to lynch him. The fact that the Pharisees were arguing with him publicly in 8:11 indicates that they are much bolder now. And not only would Jesus be in danger (remember that in 3:6 the Pharisees conspire with the Herodians to destroy him), but his followers would be as well.

A few years ago, Richard Bauckham authored a terrific book entitled *Jesus and the Eyewitnesses*. One of the fascinating points that he makes relates to some of the unnamed persons in the Gospels. He argues that in some instances those persons were still alive at the time of writing, and the Jewish establishment was hunting them down to kill them. In John's Gospel, for example, we read the following: "When the great crowd of the Jews learned that he [Jesus] was there, they came, not only on account of Jesus but also to see Laz′arus, whom he had raised from the dead. So the chief priests planned to put Laz′arus also to death, because on account of him many of the Jews were going away and believing in Jesus" (John 12:9–11).

Some of these eyewitnesses to the mighty acts of Jesus had to remain anonymous, Bauckham maintains, because they were at risk. We might think of the Gospel writers' withholding of their identity as a witness protection program. It would have been a matter of life or death.

Not much comical about that.

1. Jesus appears to heal this man in two takes. Of what significance is this detail? Of what significance is the man's response in 8:24, "I see men; but they look like trees, walking"?

2. How might this scene make more sense in light of the previous scene? (Consider the emphases on faith and understanding.)

3. How does Bauckham's suggestion impact your reading of this passage?

4. Do you feel at risk as a Christian? If so, how?

COMMENTARY NOTES

Day 2. In today's world, we sometimes use the word *hypocrite* to describe a person whose words and actions don't match up. The underlying Greek word points to a "play-actor," or someone who appears on stage wearing a mask. When we claim to be one thing, yet act contrary to what we say, we create masks for ourselves. Jesus often calls people out for their hypocritical behavior. Nowhere do we see a more extensive and devastating critique of hypocrisy by Jesus than in Matthew 23.

Day 2. Josephus was a Jewish commander who oversaw a Jewish military unit in the area of Galilee just a few years after Jesus. Because he felt that the Roman Empire actually offered the Jews hope for a peaceful existence (known as the *Pax Romana*, or "Peace of Rome"), he opposed Jewish rebellious factions. When Jews revolted against Roman rule in Jerusalem in the late AD 60s, Josephus was enlisted by Rome to negotiate a peaceful settlement with the Jewish factions. When the rebels refused, Josephus denounced their decision. As a result, Rome laid siege to the city over a period of about four years, eventually breaching its walls and razing the city and temple in AD 70. Josephus was later hired by the Roman Empire to chronicle the events of the war. His histories of the Jewish people and their wars are immensely important to our understanding of the New Testament era. These histories have been translated into English and are fascinating to read.

WEEK SIX

GATHERING DISCUSSION OUTLINE

A. Open session in prayer. Ask for specific celebrations of God's goodness.

B. What new insights have you gained from this week's readings? What has encouraged you? What has challenged you?

C. View video for this week's readings.

D. Discuss questions selected from daily readings.

1. **KEY OBSERVATION:** We sometimes require of Christians more than God requires of Christians.

   DISCUSSION QUESTION: Think of some unspoken rules that church communities sometimes maintain. These might include dress codes or prohibitions against social activities. How might they be stricter than God's biblical commands?

2. **KEY OBSERVATION:** Making God's laws stricter can be a way of honoring God, in some cases.

   DISCUSSION QUESTION: Where do you see that church doctrines or rules create a hedge of protection around God's laws? How can they be helpful and God-honoring?

3. **KEY OBSERVATION:** The problem arises when we lose sight of the *spirit* of the law for the sake of its *letter*.

   DISCUSSION QUESTION: Can you identify a church practice that seems to have no real purpose or meaning? If so, what is it? Why is it maintained? How might the practice be reconnected to an original intent or purpose? Said differently, how might the *letter* of the practice be brought back into alignment with its original *spirit*?

4. **KEY OBSERVATION:** An overemphasis on the letter of the law can have viral consequences.

   DISCUSSION QUESTION: For Jesus' disciples, short-term memory loss (Jesus had just fed thousands with one sack full of groceries) resulted in a moment of worry about what they would eat. Jesus then compared their lack of faith to the Pharisees' commitment to human traditions, describing the larger effect as that of leaven. When in your life has a failure to trust in God grown to crisis proportions? What impact did that have on you and those around you?

5. **KEY OBSERVATION:** Viral ideas can be deadly.

   DISCUSSION QUESTION: Whom do you know who has been emotionally or spiritually injured by a church practice or policy that was enforced in letter but not in spirit? What were the circumstances? How might the circumstance have been avoided or better handled?

E. What facts and information presented in the commentary portion of the lesson help you understand the weekly Scripture?

F. Close session with prayer. Ask for specific concerns to be brought before our Lord.

WEEK SEVEN

Mark 8:27–10:52

A Dark Twist to the Plot

INTRODUCTION

Our Scripture reading this week takes a very dark turn. Jesus begins to prepare his disciples for the unthinkable.

The traveling Jewish teacher whom the disciples had been following around the Galilean countryside; the mighty one who raises the dead, heals the sick, and gives sight to the blind; the wise one who teaches with unprecedented authority and offers forgiveness for sins; *this One* reveals that he is on a journey to his death at the hands of his enemies.

After establishing with great clarity that Jesus was exactly who he appeared to be, he begins to bring his disciples into the inner secret: the anointed Son of God was soon to be executed at the hands of angry men.

As you can imagine, such a word could only have been received by the disciples with mutters of, "What was that? What did he say? Did we hear that right?" Peter, in particular, finds this to be ludicrous. "Hold it, hold it, Jesus. You got that wrong. You don't die in this story. You're awesome. You're the good guy. That's not fair. You're messing up the story; now get it right!"

Jesus affirms—three times, in fact—that his way was indeed a way to death. The disciples would simply have to trust him on that.

Further, to be followers of Jesus requires a willingness to pursue a similar way, making themselves available to the ultimate will of God. In fact, disciples of Jesus must humbly submit to the authority and will of God's ultimate plan in ways that one would expect a child to accept authority. Jesus holds up children as models of Jesus' ideal disciple: "Truly, I say to you, unless you turn and become like children, you will never enter the kingdom of heaven" (Matt. 18:3).

ONE

"You Are the Christ"

Mark 8:27–29 *And Jesus went on with his disciples, to the villages of Caesare'a Philippi; and on the way he asked his disciples, "Who do men say that I am?"* *[28]And they told him, "John the Baptist; and others say, Eli'jah; and others one of the prophets." [29]And he asked them, "But who do you say that I am?" Peter answered him, "You are the Christ."*

Understanding the Word. Imagine picking up a travel magazine while you're waiting to see the doctor. Further imagine that you thumb through it to an intriguing article about America's best places to live. One category is "Best Places to Raise a Family."

What would be your impression if a community named Mayberry, North Carolina, appeared in the top slot as America's best place to raise a family? Assuming for a moment that Mayberry were a real town and there actually were such a place, would you be surprised?

Now imagine that, instead of Mayberry, North Carolina, you saw that the article recommended Las Vegas, Nevada, as America's best place to raise a family. Would you be more or less surprised than if you had seen Mayberry, North Carolina, listed? (That's probably a pretty obvious question.)

My point is this: places have reputations. Certain locales, such as cities, conjure up notions, images, and impressions. One can merely refer to a particular city, and a set of thoughts is immediately invoked. For instance, one might think of chocolate at the mention of Hershey, Pennsylvania. Or one might think of conservative, midwestern values at the mention of Ottumwa, Iowa. Or one might envision Thoroughbreds thundering across the bluegrass at the mention of Lexington, Kentucky, or alien vessels and conspiracy theories for Roswell, New Mexico.

In today's passage, Mark identifies the locale of Jesus and his disciples as Caesarea Philippi. This was a city renamed by Herod Philip II to honor Caesar Augustus. Not a bad political move.

New Testament scholar Ben Witherington (who also served as my dissertation supervisor) has an interesting perspective on the identification of this city in Mark's narrative. He notes that the city had an ancient heritage as a city named Paneas, named for the Greek god Pan (meaning "all"). Residents originally established a pagan shrine there in honor of Pan, and in later years rededicated the shrine in honor of the pagan god Baal. By the time of Mark's writing, the shrine had been repurposed to honor the Roman emperor in advancement of the imperial cult.

Dr. Witherington's observation is keen: Jesus may have strategically chosen this place to reveal his true identity as the anointed Son of God *precisely* to contrast himself with false gods and false claims of divinity. Thus, the mention of Caesarea Philippi may have conjured up for Mark's first-century readers a strong sense of pagan worship and practices. Against such a backdrop, the divinity of Jesus would have stood in strong relief.

Peter's declaration that Jesus was the Christ stands at the center of Mark's Gospel, both in terms of its theology and its pages.

1. How important is the background setting (Caesarea Philippi) of the scene here?

2. Why would Jesus be interested in what others were saying about him? As the Son of God, wouldn't he already know?

3. Why would Jesus *specifically* ask his disciples who they thought Jesus was?

4. If someone approached you tomorrow and asked you, "Who is Jesus?" how would you answer? Who is Jesus to you?

TWO

Anointed unto Death

Mark 8:31–32 *And he began to teach them that the Son of man must suffer many things, and be rejected by the elders and the chief priests and the scribes, and be killed, and after three days rise again.* [32]*And he said this plainly. . . .*

Understanding the Word. Our story started off in Mark 1 in triumph. The long period of darkness comes to close with the arrival of the awaited One. He immediately proclaims "kingdom come" and travels through the Galilean villages and countryside recruiting followers, healing the sick, exorcising demons, and raising the dead.

Not a bad time to be alive.

Even though there are murmurings of conspiracy, Jesus seems supremely unperturbed by the threats of the Jewish establishment. The plot takes a dark and sinister turn in chapter 8 of Mark's story, however, when Jesus reveals that his life is about to come to an end.

Impossible. How can this be?! How could the Son of God be killed by human beings?

This is the first of a short series of foreshadowings in which Jesus reveals to his disciples that his end is about to come. In today's passage, and in 9:30–32 as well as 10:32–34, Jesus explains that his "way" is a journey toward suffering and death. Although he also reveals that he will be raised after three days, I don't think that quite registered with his hearers.

We've seen that the words *Messiah* and *Christ* are closely related. Both mean anointed. But what does "anointed" actually mean? The word has an important place in salvation history. When the Old Testament prophet Samuel was tasked by God to replace Israel's first king (Saul), Samuel sought such a king from Jesse's sons.

> And Samuel said to Jesse, "Are all your sons here?" And he said, "There remains yet the youngest, but behold, he is keeping the sheep." And Samuel said to Jesse, "Send and fetch him; for we will not sit down till he comes here." And he sent, and brought him in. Now he was ruddy, and had beautiful eyes, and was handsome. And the LORD said, "Arise, *anoint* him; for this is he." Then Samuel took the horn of oil, and *anointed* him in the midst of his brothers; and the Spirit of the LORD came mightily upon David from that day forward. (1 Sam. 16:11–13, emphasis added)

I've italicized the word *anoint* in the passage. In Hebrew, the word for "anointed" is *mashiyach*. In Greek, it is *christos*. In each case, we see the connections to the English words *Messiah* and *Christ*. To anoint someone in this sense is a physical act that bears larger significance. David was anointed with oil for the purpose of serving as Israel's next king. That anointing was confirmed by the Spirit of the Lord coming upon David in a mighty way. Likewise, Jesus was anointed with the Spirit's descending like a dove upon him in Mark 1:10. That anointing was confirmed by the heavenly voice when he declared his pleasure with Jesus in verse 11.

Central to Jesus' anointing, however, is a journey to death. Jesus makes this clear to his disciples . . . three times. Peter can't accept it. Peter *won't* accept. It's too hard to believe.

It's impossible.

1. Why would Mark include the statement in verse 32, "And he said this plainly"? Think especially about our earlier discussion of parables in Week 4.

2. How does Jesus' foreshadowing of his death impact you emotionally? How does this knowledge affect your reading of Mark as you go forward?

3. How does Jesus' foreshadowing of his resurrection impact you emotionally? How does *this* knowledge affect your reading of Mark as you go forward?

4. Which fact—that Jesus will die or that he will rise after three days—occupies your focus more as you move forward with your reading?

THREE

"Trust Me"

Mark 8:32–33 . . . *And Peter took him, and began to rebuke him.* ³³*But turning and seeing his disciples, he rebuked Peter, and said, "Get behind me, Satan! For you are not on the side of God, but of men."*

Understanding the Word. Sometimes things don't exactly go our way. When they don't, we sometimes wave our fists in the air and shout, "I am mad at you, God! I love you, but I am really, really mad at you right now!"

Sometimes I feel this way, usually because things aren't going my way. Sometimes I feel this way because God asks me to do something I just don't want to do. Jonah felt that way. God wanted him to go and preach a message of repentance to the people of Ninevah. It wasn't that Ninevah was such a bad place to visit. (I'm not saying I'd want to build a summer home there or anything, but some of the trees are actually quite lovely.) Jonah didn't want to go to Ninevah because he didn't *want* them to repent. He wanted things his way.

I wrestle with wanting things my way all the time. Denying our own wills isn't easy. If it were, everyone would be doing it. When God nudges us to pursue his path, we resist. Sometimes we dig in our heels. Sometimes we get angry.

I think Peter got angry because he thought Jesus was making a mistake. Or more likely, he didn't like what he was hearing. He wasn't trusting Jesus.

In the same way, our boys sometimes get angry with their mother and me. I get that. I got angry at my parents when I didn't get my way, or when they made me do something I didn't want to do. Like I said, I get that.

When I try to convince our sons that saving their money for something big might be better than wasting it on something small, I usually have a battle on my hands. They just don't understand. And it sometimes makes me angry . . . because ultimately they don't trust me. They don't trust that I might know what's better for them in the long run. If I could just make them understand. . . .

Wow, as I think about it, that must be how God feels when we don't listen . . . when we assert our own way . . . when we demand that he act according to our wishes, rather than the other way around. We must weary him to the point of frustration with our lack of trust.

I distinctly remember not wanting to leave our home in Indiana to move to Kentucky in 2004 for me to finish my seminary studies. I didn't want to go. I didn't think Indiana could get along without me. I didn't want to sever ties. My wife knew we should move. Our church leadership knew we should move. Everyone seemed to get it but me.

Looking back, I guess I really did trust God, because we did move. But I did it reluctantly, because I really didn't trust him as much as I could or should. I've seen things in the last ten years that cause me to think otherwise. God *is* reliable. Even if our worlds fall completely apart, we have to remember that as our perfect parent, God is saying gently, "Trust me."

1. When in life have you been angry at God? What were the circumstances?

2. Looking back on that circumstance, where do you see evidence of God at work or of his grace?

3. How would you encourage someone who has deep-seated anger toward God to trust him?

FOUR

Paradox

Mark 8:34–9:1 *And he called to him the multitude with his disciples, and said to them, "If any man would come after me, let him deny himself and take up his cross and follow me. ³⁵For whoever would save his life will lose it; and whoever loses his life for my sake and the gospel's will save it. ³⁶For what does it profit a man, to gain the whole world and forfeit his life? ³⁷For what can a man give in return for his life? ³⁸For whoever is ashamed of me and of my words in this adulterous and sinful generation, of him will the Son of man also be ashamed, when he comes in the glory of his Father with the holy angels."*

⁹:¹And he said to them, "Truly, I say to you, there are some standing here who will not taste death before they see that the kingdom of God has come with power."

Understanding the Word. In yesterday's reading, I'm sure that Peter thought he was acting nobly when he reacted as he did to Jesus' pronouncement that Jesus was to be killed in Jerusalem. The problem was that he failed to see the bigger picture, and in so doing, he failed to trust Jesus. Peter was operating under one set of principles: namely, that Jesus and the boys would likely have fun storming the castle, as it were, and establish Jesus on the throne in Jerusalem. Jesus, however, was operating under a different set of principles, principles that made no sense to Peter; principles that, in fact, ran counter to common sense.

To be sure, what Jesus announced was a paradox.

In the verses for today, we read about this paradox. Turning from Peter to the crowds, Jesus begins to teach them that any followers of his must be willing to abandon their own agendas, surrender their own interests, discard their own operating principles and assumptions. Jesus' perspective was a view of reality from thirty thousand feet; Peter's perspective was a view from ground zero.

In the 1940s, near the end of World War II, a young German theologian named Dietrich Bonhoeffer was hanged in a Nazi concentration camp, just days before Allied forces liberated the camp. His offense? Opposing the German national church's cooperation with the Third Reich. His opposition earned him a death sentence at a time when his career as an emerging world-class theologian should have been skyrocketing.

A few years earlier, Bonhoeffer had written a book entitled *The Cost of Discipleship*. In it, he walks his readers through the Sermon on the Mount (as recorded in the Gospel of Matthew), noting the high price of "costly" grace (grace that cost Jesus his life) as opposed to "cheap" grace that would seem to provide eternal security without any commitment from the recipient. In this landmark book, Bonhoeffer says this: "When Christ calls a man, he bids him come and die."

The coincidence is that Bonhoeffer himself would pay the ultimate price of his life for his commitment to the Jesus of Scripture. The paradox is this: in losing his life, Bonhoeffer found it. By surrendering his own assumptions about how the world ought to work, he willingly and staunchly maintained his commitment to the liberation of the Jews, knowing indeed that Jesus would have done likewise. In this, Bonhoeffer's life and writings have become a legacy for generations to come.

I remember becoming introduced to contemporary Christian music in the early nineties. An enormously popular song of that era was Steven Curtis Chapman's, "For the Sake of the Call," from an album by the same name. Interestingly, Chapman wrote the album after studying *The Cost of Discipleship*, and many of the songs on the album convey Bonhoeffer's views of costly discipleship. One of the songs on the album is about Paul, and offers this refrain: "What kind of joy is this, that counts it a blessing to suffer?"

That's a paradox.

Following Christ is a paradox: to find life, we must let go of it. Or to put it a bit more clearly: to find life as God intended, we must be willing to let go of our own demands and expectations about what life could and should look like. Only when we surrender those demands and expectations can we begin to see the kingdom come with power.

1. What might Jesus mean when he says, "whoever would save his life will lose it; and whoever loses his life for my sake and the gospel's will save it"? Is this a paradox? Why or why not?

2. As you reflect on your own journey into faith, where has the gospel required you to sacrifice something? What was the personal price of that sacrifice?

3. Do you regret the cost of discipleship? Why or why not?

FIVE

Transfiguration

Mark 9:2–4 *And after six days Jesus took with him Peter and James and John, and led them up a high mountain apart by themselves; and he was transfigured before them, ³and his garments became glistening, intensely white, as no fuller on earth could bleach them. ⁴And there appeared to them Eli'jah with Moses; and they were talking to Jesus.*

Understanding the Word. For about twenty years, Owen Dickens led a Sunday school class at my home church. He's also an Old Testament professor and a wonderful man. As I was writing this lesson, our class was working through a study of the Gospel of Mark. I so very much appreciate Owen's even-handed treatment of the Bible, his expertise in the New Testament (even though the Old Testament is his specialty), and the fresh perspectives he brings to our discussions.

In our text this week, we are moving very carefully—almost verse by verse—through this stretch in the middle of Mark's Gospel. It is indeed a pivotal piece of literary real estate. One of Owen's strengths is reading in context, meaning that he appeals to the material leading up to and following a passage to help shed light on a passage. Owen noted that many questions could arise from the transfiguration account, such as:

- Why did Jesus choose Peter, James, and John to join him? What about Andrew?
- How is "after six days" significant to the story?
- Which mountain were they on?
- Why were Moses and Elijah present?
- How did Peter, James, and John recognize that the two figures with Jesus were Elijah and Moses? (As a sidebar, one of my own professors

offered this suggestion: "Maybe Peter had a picture of them on his fridge; something like a 'heroes of the Bible' trading card, or something.")

In varying degrees, these are well-grounded questions, some for which we'll likely never have answers. But I think we can gain some traction on the significance of the account if we read the passage in context. Consider the following.

First, Jesus had for the first time announced that he was heading to Jerusalem for an untimely death. Second, Peter took issue with that statement, then Jesus took issue with Peter. Third, Jesus explains that following him requires something of a paradox. However, those who do follow him will not die before they see "the kingdom . . . come with power" (9:1).

So how might the transfiguration be understood within this flow of events?

I suspect that Jesus was fully aware how incredibly difficult his announcement must have been for Peter to hear. Peter—or any of the others, for that matter—would not have been able to wrap his mind around that at all. As a way of encouraging Peter in particular, Jesus invites Peter and two eyewitnesses (James and John) to catch a glimpse of the proverbial light at the end of the tunnel. With a vision of Jesus' potential glory, Peter and the others could move forward in confidence knowing that the end would justify the means, even if they didn't have every detail worked out.

The voice declaring from the heavens in Mark 1 that Jesus was his beloved Son is the same voice that thunders from the cloud, "This is my beloved Son; listen to him" (Mark 9:7).

1. For today's reflections, consider the questions raised above. Spend some time thinking about possible answers to those questions or ways you could explore possible answers through your own research. Where might you go to seek answers?

COMMENTARY NOTES

Day 1. When Rome began its occupation of Palestine in the first century BC, the government enlisted the support of local rulers to administer justice, collect taxes, and maintain peace. Through shrewd political maneuvering, Herod the Great earned an appointment as the client king over the Jews. In effect, he was a puppet king serving Roman interests. Upon his death just after the birth of Jesus (Herod is a key figure in the second chapter of Matthew), his jurisdiction was divided into four primary areas of rule (a "tetrarchy"), each overseen by one of his sons. One son, Herod Archelaus, ruled over two regions. The other two sons given rule were Herod Antipas (who beheaded John the Baptist in Mark 6) and Herod Philip II, also known as Philip the Tetrarch. When Philip rose to power, he renamed the city Caesarea Philippi as a means of honoring the Roman emperor, Caesar Augustus.

Day 1. Caesar Augustus was the Roman emperor enthroned at the time of Jesus. He was the second in the line of Caesars, the first being Julius Caesar, who rose to power as Rome transitioned from a republic governed by a senate to an empire governed by one individual. The Caesars maintained their role in the empire through the early part of the second century (about one hundred years after the life of Jesus). Over time, the Caesars came to be worshiped as divine and, at times, systematically persecuted Christians.

Day 1. The imperial cult refers to the worship of Caesar as a human governing with divine authority.

Day 2. *Foreshadowing* is a literary term that refers to an author's subtle hint that something will happen in the future. Here, Mark quotes Jesus as declaring that he would be killed. This is arguably more than a subtle foreshadowing, but nevertheless casts a somber tone over the rest of Mark's narrative as the reader anticipates the eventual death of Jesus.

Day 4. A paradox is a seeming contradiction. In this case, it is the pairing of two statements or assertions that seem in logical opposition to one another.

WEEK SEVEN

GATHERING DISCUSSION OUTLINE

A. Open session in prayer. Ask for specific celebrations of God's goodness.

B. What new insights have you gained from this week's readings? What has encouraged you? What has challenged you?

C. View video for this week's readings.

D. Discuss questions selected from daily readings.

1. **KEY OBSERVATION:** Mark's mention of geography underscores the difference between Jesus as the Son of God and false, earthly claims of divinity.

   DISCUSSION QUESTION: Suppose that Jesus lived with us today instead of two thousand years ago. Where do you think he would choose to reveal his identity? Why?

2. **KEY OBSERVATION:** Jesus, as *anointed* Son of God, was destined to die.

   DISCUSSION QUESTION: Recall from an earlier lesson that the word *Christ* means "anointed." How does your perception of the word *Christ* change knowing that Jesus was anointed to die? What feelings does that evoke in you?

3. **KEY OBSERVATION:** Even though God's purposes seem crazy to us, he is trustworthy.

   DISCUSSION QUESTION: When in life have you been angry at God? What were the circumstances? (This question may require members of the group to reopen old wounds. Please don't feel compelled to share anything you're not comfortable sharing. As other members share, please don't judge them for how they dealt with their anger toward God.) Where have you seen evidence of his trustworthiness despite those circumstances?

4. **KEY OBSERVATION:** The paradox is this: in order to gain our lives, we must lose them.

   DISCUSSION QUESTION: In what areas of life is God calling you to take a risk? Are you unwilling to let go and trust God? If so, what is holding you back?

5. **KEY OBSERVATION:** The transfiguration served to encourage Jesus' followers by giving them a vision of God's outcome.

   DISCUSSION QUESTION: Consider how the transfiguration followed after Jesus' foreshadowing of his death and his paradoxical teaching. Consider also how it provided the disciples a vision worth striving toward. How does your vision of God's future glory encourage (or discourage) you in your daily walk with him?

E. What facts and information presented in the commentary portion of the lesson help you understand the weekly Scripture?

F. Close session with prayer. Ask for specific concerns to be brought before our Lord.

WEEK EIGHT

Mark 11:1–12:12

Parable of the Wicked Tenants

INTRODUCTION

This parable serves as the central focus of Jesus' triumphal entry into Jerusalem. In it, he identifies himself as the beloved son who is rejected by the wicked tenants. Of course, the point of the parable is not about tenants and landowners, but about the religious establishment and God's chosen representatives.

The parable is situated within the final week of Jesus' life. The essential chain of events through the first four days are as follows:

- Palm Sunday—Jesus dispatches messengers to arrange for transportation. The transportation turns out to be a donkey. Jesus mounts the donkey and heads to Jerusalem amid shouts of triumph from the crowd. He proceeds to the temple, where he conducts a tour. He then withdraws to Bethany, just outside the city, where he camps for the night with his colleagues.
- Monday—Jesus heads back into the city. On the way, he seeks some fruit from a fig tree. Finding none, he curses the fig tree. He then goes on into the city and pulls a surprise inspection of the temple, where he chases out the money-changers and vendors. Drawing the anger of the temple officials, he retreats back to his base camp for another night outside the city.
- Tuesday—Jesus returns to the city for a third straight day. On the way this time, the disciples observe that the fig tree had withered, creating a yet-to-be-understood depiction of the state of affairs in the temple. Jesus claims the opportunity to teach about faith and forgiveness.

- Wednesday—As Jesus comes into Jerusalem for a fourth straight day, members of the religious establishment confront him and demand to see his credentials. Jesus, however, responds with a parable in which he characterizes the religious leaders as wicked tenants who withhold from their landowner what is rightfully his.

ONE

Palm Sunday

Mark 11:1–4 *And when they drew near to Jerusalem, to Beth'phage and Bethany, at the Mount of Olives, he sent two of his disciples, ²and said to them, "Go into the village opposite you, and immediately as you enter it you will find a colt tied, on which no one has ever sat; untie it and bring it. ³If any one says to you, 'Why are you doing this?' say, 'The Lord has need of it and will send it back here immediately.'" ⁴And they went away, and found a colt tied at the door out in the open street; and they untied it.*

Understanding the Word. Jesus appears to be supremely in command of the circumstances around him. He's just indicated to his disciples that his journey into Jerusalem was ultimately a journey to his death. Now he seems to be making arrangements to set that horrible drama in motion. He knows that everything is in place and ready for the time prepared for him. And as a dutiful Son, he walks squarely into the face of imminent danger.

The colt was the vehicle by which Jesus was to enter Jerusalem. What a contrast to our president's arrival in *Air Force One*. What a contrast to an Oscar nominee's arrival in a limousine. What a contrast to Pharaoh's arrival in a chariot. The true King is about to enter the Holy City . . . on a jackass.

What a contrast.

The people likely knew the symbolism of this act. It was a sign to indicate that Messiah had arrived and was ready to ascend to his throne. Jesus is met in verses 9–10 with shouts of acclamation. In place of today's red carpet, the people take off their jackets and cut off palm branches, laying them before the King as a way of receiving him.

The script is being followed perfectly . . .

Rejoice greatly, O daughter of Zion! Shout aloud, O daughter of Jerusalem! Lo, your king comes to you; triumphant and victorious is he, humble and riding on an ass, on a colt the foal of an ass. (Zech. 9:9)

The occasion was the annual celebration of Passover. Thousands upon thousands would ascend Mt. Zion to the City of David at its summit. It was a high and holy festival. It was exciting, noisy, dirty, bustling, and filled with anticipation.

But what an irony from Jesus' perspective. The holy temple, one of the seven wonders of the world, the dwelling place of the Holy God of Israel . . . had become a shopping mall. Vendors, merchants, and kiosks were everywhere. What had been established as holy had been completely profaned, or made common. Jesus went ballistic, screaming at the retailers, chasing them with a whip, and flipping over their tables.

This is an unusual and seldom-discussed side of Jesus' nature. Perhaps part of his frustration stemmed from the fact that not only was the temple no longer a house of prayer for all nations, but it represented an establishment that had largely closed itself to the abiding voice of God. Despite a steady string of messengers having been sent by God to warn Jerusalem of its unfaithfulness, the Holy City was about to crucify the Son of the Most High. The city ready to receive him as King with palm branches and shouts of "Hosannah!" is the same city that is about to torture and brutally execute him.

1. What about today's passage suggests that Jesus is supremely in command of the circumstances around him? Refer back to the passage.

2. What is significant about the fact that the colt had never been sat upon?

3. What is the tone of this passage (relaxed, tense, desperate, comical, etc.)? What words or phrases lead you to that conclusion?

TWO

Triumph

Mark 11:7–9 *And they brought the colt to Jesus, and threw their garments on it; and he sat upon it. ⁸And many spread their garments on the road, and others spread leafy branches which they had cut from the fields. ⁹And those who went before and those who followed cried out, "Hosanna! Blessed is he who comes in the name of the Lord!"*

Understanding the Word. In yesterday's lesson, we observed how Jesus seemed supremely in control of his circumstances. His requisition of a donkey's colt is part of the unfolding drama, and it sets the stage for a very unexpected and unlikely way for a king to enter his city. In the passage for today, we learn of the crowds' response to their King.

A bit of background may add to the significance of the scene.

These events take place under the shadow of Rome, whose empire stretched across most of the Mediterranean world. A long-standing tradition of Rome was to honor its military commanders with a parade upon his return from victorious battle. Such battles usually involved a quest for foreign lands and resources to satisfy Rome's appetite for more territories.

The commander would march his army to the outskirts of Rome, and hold there while he dispatched messengers into the city to request a triumph. A triumph was an honor bestowed upon such military commanders by consent of the senate and significantly elevated the status and power of the commander. As such, a triumph held enormous political implications for those involved.

Once bestowed, the Roman senate would announce the particulars of the triumph to the Roman citizens, who would then make preparations for the procession. At the appointed time, the commander would enter the city in a chariot drawn by four horses. He would wear the ceremonial toga (white robe) and laurel (green garland). His unarmed forces would accompany him along with the spoils of conquest, including captured soldiers. As a final act, the captured soldiers would be executed.

It is important to note that the commander's forces would enter the city unarmed. In fact, the commander and his army would not enter the city until given permission by the senate to do so. The period of waiting could be quite long at times as Roman politicians considered the commander's request for the triumph, evaluated the possible outcomes of various decisions, and brokered the deal to make it happen. If the commander were to enter the city without permission and with armed forces, it would most likely have been viewed as a hostile act.

The significance of this background information lies in its connection to Jesus' entry into Jerusalem. Note the contrast. The commander enters in a chariot. Jesus enters on a donkey. The commander encamps outside the city with his armed forces. Jesus encamps outside the city with his inner circle of twelve. The commander executes his opponents. Jesus willingly consents to his own execution.

Just as we noted in yesterday's lesson, what a contrast!

1. Why would Mark include details about the people's garments? How is this important?

2. How does the background information about the ceremonial Roman triumph contribute to your understanding of today's passage? What other questions does the information raise, or what would you like to research further?

3. Knowing that Jerusalem and its surrounding regions were under direct governance of Rome, how dangerous would it have been to celebrate Jesus in this way? What would it likely mean for Jesus to come "in the name of the Lord"?

THREE

Grapes of Wrath

Isaiah 5:1–4, 7 *Let me sing for my beloved a love song concerning his vineyard: My beloved had a vineyard on a very fertile hill. ²He digged it and cleared it of stones, and planted it with choice vines; he built a watchtower in the midst of it, and hewed out a wine vat in it; and he looked for it to yield grapes, but it yielded wild grapes.*

³And now, O inhabitants of Jerusalem and men of Judah, judge, I pray you, between me and my vineyard. ⁴What more was there to do for my vineyard, that I have not done in it? When I looked for it to yield grapes, why did it yield wild grapes? . . .

⁷For the vineyard of the Lord of hosts is the house of Israel, and the men of Judah are his pleasant planting; and he looked for justice, but behold, bloodshed; for righteousness, but behold, a cry!

Understanding the Word. You will recall from Week 1 that Isaiah is our true north in Mark's Gospel. It is the point to which we fix our reading. Isaiah prophesied that Jerusalem would "mutate" into an unholy fruit. He also prophesied that God will not tolerate such unholiness, but will instead bring the multiplication of that fruit to an end. Jesus' reinterpretation of the parable in this week's reading makes the same point.

Isaiah, writing at a time when Israel was under attack by foreign empires, challenged God's people—especially their religious leaders—to establish justice. Those in power were abusing that power, seeking personal gain and status over fairness and equity.

The image of the vineyard is a powerful one. When God called Abraham in Genesis 12 to "Go," Abraham left a prosperous, secure existence. God promised that he would lead Abraham to a "land flowing with milk and honey." At first, that land seemed to be the northern part of Egypt, in a region called Goshen. There, in the lush and fertile delta of the Nile River, God's people multiplied greatly. Relations with Egypt were good, and the people prospered.

Four hundred years later, a new Egyptian king sat on the throne. He feared the size and strength of the Hebrews, and instituted a system of forced slavery that would bring this era of prosperity to a halt. Under the leadership of Moses, God led his people from Egyptian bondage to that final destination of a "land flowing with milk and honey": Canaan (see Exodus 3:8, 17; 13:5; and 33:3 for just a few of the many references). That journey should have been a short journey of just a few weeks. However, the repeated lack of trust in God resulted in a forty-year delay of that entry for God's people.

When that generation of faithless souls passed, the Hebrews were able to enter Canaan and claim it for their own. It was the lush region of what is known as the Fertile Crescent, an area of rich land nursed by fresh water streams and rivers. It was to be their vineyard.

An interesting thing about vineyards is that they take time to establish—years, in fact. That a society is able to enjoy the fruit of the vine indicates that they have established themselves, and they are stable. The vineyard imagery in Isaiah represents that God's work of creating a suitable habitat for his people is complete. The careful attention to detail (clearing stones, planting with choice vines, building a watchtower, digging a vat) reminds us of God's careful attention to detail in the opening moments of creation in Genesis 1. God painstakingly creates an environment in which his commandment to "be fruitful and multiply" (Gen. 1:22) can become reality.

God's vineyard was designed to sustain his people . . . *all* of them. But in the time of Isaiah, the religious leaders were abusing their roles and depriving the common people of what should have rightfully been theirs. And God takes a rather dim view of injustice.

This parable in Isaiah is *central* to understanding the parable Jesus tells in tomorrow's lesson.

1. Make a close and careful comparison of the parable in Isaiah 5 with the parable in Mark 12. How are they similar? How are they different?

2. If Jesus wanted to criticize the religious establishment, why wouldn't he come right out and do so? Why would he have chosen the indirect method of criticizing them with a parable?

3. If you have time, make a close and careful comparison of the details in Isaiah 5 and Mark 12 (especially the opening verses) with Genesis 1. What similarities exist?

FOUR

The Divine Drama (Part 1)

Mark 12:2–6 *"When the time came, he sent a servant to the tenants, to get from them some of the fruit of the vineyard. ³And they took him and beat him, and sent him away empty-handed. ⁴Again he sent to them another servant, and they wounded him in the head, and treated him shamefully. ⁵And he sent another, and*

*him they killed; and so with many others, some they beat and some they killed.
⁶He had still one other, a beloved son; finally he sent him to them, saying, 'They
will respect my son.'"*

Understanding the Word. Recall from Week 1 that Mark's prologue was a
run-up to the life and teaching of Jesus. In effect, it is a review of the divine
drama up to and including the moment when God chooses to send his Son, his
beloved . . . advanced by a messenger, and receiving divine affirmation. Note
these verses from the prologue:

> "Behold, I send my messenger before thy face, who shall prepare thy way."
> (Mark 1:2)

> A voice came from heaven, "Thou art my beloved Son; with thee I am well
> pleased." (Mark 1:11)

> "The time is fulfilled, and the kingdom of God is at hand . . ." (Mark 1:15)

I suspect that Mark probably had this parable of the wicked tenants in
mind when he set about writing his prologue. As the recording secretary for
Peter, Mark would have used as the starting point for Peter's journey with Jesus
the passage beginning at 1:16, where Jesus sees and then invites Peter to lay
down his nets. Further, Mark would have Peter's notes and accounts available
to him as he crafted the prologue to his Gospel.

The connection between the two accounts—that of the prologue and that
of the parable of the wicked tenants—couldn't be clearer. For the parable, the
background is the intentional and creative work of the owner of the vineyard prior to his leaving the country. For the prologue, the background is the
off-stage conversation between the Father and the Son in the Isaiah citation.

For the parable, the representatives sent to the tenants are the owner's
agents, who are abused and even killed by the wicked tenants. For the prologue,
the representatives are John the Baptist, specifically, but the entire prophetic
tradition (including Isaiah) in general. Note that John's arrest serves as the
prelude to the climactic words of Jesus in 1:15, and that John's death at the
hands of Herod is recounted in Mark 6:16–28.

For the parable, the son of the owner is sent to collect the owner's share,
and he is described as "beloved" in 12:6. For the prologue, the Son of the

Father is sent to proclaim the good news and issue a call to repentance and right belief. He, too, is described as "beloved" (1:11).

Mark would have written in light of Jesus' death and resurrection. In fact, he chronicles those events in chapters 15 and 16 (which we'll examine in the final week of this study). Thus, Mark's prologue sets the stage for the sending of the Son, and explains—in part, perhaps—why a sane businessman like Peter would walk away from his livelihood: because this is the One, *the anointed Son of God*. And perhaps more important, Mark knows the end of the story, specifically that Jesus triumphs over the grave, making Jesus' advent on earth—despite his way of the cross—*good news*.

1. Because of the close relationship between the parable of the wicked tenants in Mark 12 and Mark's prologue in chapter 1, it may be helpful to take a moment and reread Mark 1:1–15.

2. After doing so, how significant is the parable of the wicked tenants for Mark's Gospel both in terms of its message and its location in Mark?

FIVE

The Divine Drama (Part 2)

Mark 12:9–11 *"What will the owner of the vineyard do? He will come and destroy the tenants, and give the vineyard to others. ¹⁰Have you not read this Scripture: 'The very stone which the builders rejected has become the head of the corner; ¹¹this was the Lord's doing, and it is marvelous in our eyes'?"*

Understanding the Word. The parable of the wicked tenants is significant in Mark for at least a couple of reasons. First, it represents a triggering moment in which Jesus' opponents are moved to action. Without saying it directly, the point of Jesus' parable is obvious: the religious leaders *are* those wicked tenants, and Jesus reveals their future. In response, they attempt to arrest him, but are prevented by the crowds. No longer are they simply planning to destroy him; now they are actively looking for an opportunity.

Second, and perhaps unlike any other parable, this one is a *totalizing* parable. It stretches from end to end of the divine drama. It reaches back to the beginning moments of salvation history when God was engaged in his meticulous, creative work. It covers the long period of Old Testament history during which time God repeatedly sent prophets and messengers to remind Israel who her true King is. It brings us to the moment in which God chooses to send his Son, whose destiny is to be rejected by the tenants. It then culminates in final judgment when the tenants are removed from power and the vineyard is given over to honorable and faithful tenants.

This is a parable ultimately about the grand sweep of the divine drama, culminating in God's righteous judgment. As such, it is situated as the controlling parable for the whole of Mark. In a few short words, Jesus is able to clearly and carefully explain the entire course of human history, and his role in it.

Jesus makes it clear that overseeing the vineyard is not a *right* to be assumed on the basis of one's family lineage or social standing. Rather, it is a *privilege* for those who faithfully serve the master's wish. In the absence of the master, the stewards are expected to obediently conduct their daily work, being sure to share the proceeds according to the will of the master.

In Jesus' time, however, those stewards were unwilling to submit their control, their earnings, and their status to the will of the vineyard-owner. When Jesus showed up as the duly authorized representative of the King himself, the stewards made hasty plans to dispose of him, and rid themselves of his pesky nuisance.

No matter how grave the drama seems to become, Jesus remains steady. He's following the script. He knows how the story ends. That doesn't mean that he faces his way with exuberance or glee; rather, he faces it with quiet obedience in the full confidence that God is faithful.

1. In what way do you see this parable as a *totalizing* story of God's salvation history?

2. In the final week's video, I will provide a discussion of how the divine drama (the biblical narrative of salvation history) is presented in a number of acts. The acts are the stories of (1) creation, (2) the fall, (3) Israel, (4) Jesus, (5) the church, and (6) new creation. How helpful is this description?

3. What is your role in this divine drama? Where do you see yourself and/or your church as actors on this stage?

COMMENTARY NOTES

General Comments. During the time of Jesus, a great gap existed between the wealthy and the poor. There was, in reality, no middle class. Only the wealthy owned land, and they accumulated more wealth by leasing their land to tenant farmers who farmed the ground under contract. By requiring high percentages of the farmers' earnings as payment for use of the land, landowners were able to maintain and even increase their holdings. Meanwhile, tenant farmers worked hard to maintain even a modest existence. Their circumstances became even more difficult during periods of drought, plague, or warfare.

General Comments. Because tenant farmers relied on the produce of their land for their earnings, they had no steady stream of income like a weekly or monthly paycheck. Their earnings for the year would come in one lump sum at the time of harvest when their crops were sold at market. Ideally, market conditions would be favorable and farmers would receive a good price for their crops. However, and as mentioned in the previous note, environmental and political conditions could adversely affect the price of their produce. Landowners often lived remotely (usually in cities away from the lower class peasant farmers) and would thus send agents to collect lease payments from the farmers. Failure on the part of the farmers to pay the agreed upon percentage could lead to harsh consequences, including eviction from the land. Once removed from the land, farmers and their families would have no means of subsistence and could therefore face possible starvation.

The agents hired by landowners served in a capacity similar to collection agents today. They were highly motivated to collect what was due the landowners since a portion of those revenues would be paid to the agents as a commission. By sending his son, the landowner in the parable sends a representative that has authority beyond the agents—the son is in fact the heir of the estate. If the son dies (within the narrative of the parable), no heir would remain and the estate would presumably enter probate. The parable itself seems to presume that the tenant farmers would somehow receive the land by legal means.

Here we see Jesus drawing heavily on the reality that tenant farmers face when they fail to live into agreements established with landowners. The gravity of this outcome in the parable would be very real to Jesus' listening audience.

Day 1. "Hosanna" comes from a Hebrew or Aramaic phrase meaning *help*. Here and elsewhere in the New Testament (the word appears in Matthew 21:9, 15; Mark 11:9–10; and John 12:13), the phrase can be understood as something like, "Please save us!" or simply "Help!"

Day 4. This could be a reference to one of two individuals in the prophetic tradition: Elisha (2 Kings 2:23–24) or John the Baptist (Mark 6:17–29).

WEEK EIGHT

GATHERING DISCUSSION OUTLINE

A. Open session in prayer. Ask for specific celebrations of God's goodness.

B. What new insights have you gained from this week's readings? What has encouraged you? What has challenged you?

C. View video for this week's readings.

D. Discuss questions selected from daily readings.

1. **KEY OBSERVATION:** Jesus was in control of his circumstances.

   DISCUSSION QUESTION: To what degree do you think Jesus was free to choose his own destiny? Do you think he had the freedom to comply with or reject God's plan? Why or why not?

2. **KEY OBSERVATION:** Jesus' "triumphal entry" stood in sharp contrast to that of the prevailing imperial culture.

   DISCUSSION QUESTION: As you consider religious and political leaders today, how would you characterize their humility and commitment toward serving others? What lesson does Jesus teach us here in practical terms?

3. **KEY OBSERVATION:** Isaiah's parable of the vineyard undergirds Jesus' parable of the wicked tenants.

   DISCUSSION QUESTION: As you consider the vineyard of your local church, is it producing delicious fruit or sour grapes? How so?

4. **KEY OBSERVATION:** The parable of the wicked tenants bears a strong relationship to Mark's prologue.

   DISCUSSION QUESTION: Assuming that Mark penned his prologue (1:1–15) as a way of introducing Peter's memoirs (1:16 and following), what might the main point of Mark's Gospel be, especially in light of the parable of the wicked tenants?

5. **KEY OBSERVATION:** The parable of the wicked tenants is a totalizing parable that captures the full span of salvation history.

   DISCUSSION QUESTION: What is your role in this divine drama? Where do you see yourself and/or your church as actors on this stage?

E. What facts and information presented in the commentary portion of the lesson help you understand the weekly Scripture?

F. Close session with prayer. Ask for specific concerns to be brought before our Lord.

WEEK NINE

Mark 12:13–40

Jewish Responses to the Prevailing Culture

INTRODUCTION

At times the New Testament world can seem rather foreign to us. It uses lots of words, mentions lots of places, and describes lots of customs that we simply don't understand. The passage for this week is typical. In it we encounter Pharisees, Herodians, Sadducees, scribes, Caesar, taxes, foreign currency, and ancient marriage customs, just to name a few. But what does all this mean?

One of our tasks as *better* readers of the Bible is to read it in *context*; that is, to understand the world of that time and to read with that world in mind. Or to put it differently, to read in context is to hear the story as it would be understood by its original audience.

The ministry of Jesus likely took place sometime around AD 30. The location was Palestine, a strategic little crossroads at the eastern edge of the Mediterranean, and connecting Europe, Asia, and Africa. That part of the world was largely occupied by the Roman Empire during that time, an empire that contracted with local authorities to administer justice, manage the economy, and promote civil order. This is the circumstance of Jesus' day, and for most Jews, it was a problem . . . a really big problem.

Dating clear back to the time of Genesis 12, God had promised and renewed his promise to fashion a people for himself. Beginning with Abraham, God raised up for himself a people named Israel who were not only to be his chosen people, but a light to the world. Israel—like nearly all people—struggled with obedience, though. The typical cycle went something like this: God would bless his people, they would prosper, they would sin, God would punish them, they would repent, and God would bless them. This cycle repeated itself over, and over, and over again. This, in fact, constitutes most of the Old Testament story.

Around the year 587 BC, this cycle reached an unfortunate climax of sorts. Because of the faithlessness of Israel's kings, the nation had splintered into two less-defensible kingdoms. The northern kingdom fell to Assyria around 722 BC. The southern kingdom fell to Babylon in 587 BC. And not only did the southern kingdom fall, but the city of Jerusalem was sacked and the temple was destroyed. Further, the best and brightest of the Israelites were exiled to Babylon for a period of about seventy years. During that time, the people lamented, "But what about God's promise?"

God's people did eventually repent and were restored to their homeland. However, the face of Judaism changed forever as the people of God reacted in very different ways to the surrounding pagan culture of their day. Some embraced that culture; some fought it; some withdrew from it; but some tried to live obediently in the midst of it.

ONE

The Accommodators

Mark 12:18–23 *And Sadducees came to him, who say that there is no resurrection; and they asked him a question, saying,* ¹⁹*"Teacher, Moses wrote for us that if a man's brother dies and leaves a wife, but leaves no child, the man must take the wife, and raise up children for his brother.* ²⁰*There were seven brothers; the first took a wife, and when he died left no children;* ²¹*and the second took her, and died, leaving no children; and the third likewise;* ²²*and the seven left no children. Last of all the woman also died.* ²³*In the resurrection whose wife will she be? For the seven had her as wife."*

Understanding the Word. In this passage, Mark provides us with a clarifying comment that he senses will be necessary for at least some members of his potential audience. Note that in verse 18 he offers this parenthetical comment about the Sadducees: ". . . who say that there is no resurrection . . ." This comment is the key to understanding what follows, if the reader does not have a working knowledge of the beliefs of the Saducean party.

At the time of Mark's writing, Palestine had become a mix of cultural beliefs and ideologies. Most dominant was the Hellenistic culture of the earlier Greek Empire. That program was further modified and advanced by the Roman Empire in place during the era of the New Testament. As mentioned briefly in Week 6, Hellenization brought with it new ways of thinking and living: Jerusalem was reorganized on the basis of the Greek *polis* (or "city"), roads and ports were built, educational systems were established, and the arts flourished. For many progressive-thinking Jews, this was a welcome advance.

Those who tended to accommodate the advancing Hellenism were typically the wealthy, urban elites. They were closely connected to the temple and its practices, and remained committed to the Torah solely, rejecting the oral interpretations of the Pharisees. Further, they believed strongly in human free will, and did not believe in an afterlife (as our Scripture indicates). These principles, among others, distinguish the Sadducees from other Jewish elements. Of course, not all Sadducees remained committed to each principle in equal measure. Some were a bit more cautious in their embrace of Hellenism.

On the other hand, some Jews adopted the advance of Hellenism to such a degree that they even sought to disassociate themselves from Jewish customs and practices. For example, one of the innovations of Hellenism was the *gymnasium*, roughly equivalent to a college preparatory school today. As part of the curriculum, pupils engaged in a program of physical education. Part of that educational program involved Greek wrestling, which was done in the nude. Some Jewish pupils came to be embarrassed by their marks of circumcision, and sought surgical means of reversing those marks. Although a part of the apocryphal books of the Bible, 1 Maccabees is enormously helpful to us in portraying the world at that time:

> In those days lawless men came forth from Israel, and misled many, saying, "Let us go and make a covenant with the Gentiles round about us, for since we separated from them many evils have come upon us." This proposal pleased them, and some of the people eagerly went to the king. He authorized them to observe the ordinances of the Gentiles.
>
> So they built a gymnasium in Jerusalem, according to Gentile custom, and removed the marks of circumcision, and abandoned the holy covenant. They joined with the Gentiles and sold themselves to do evil. (1 Macc. 1:11–15)

Clearly, this author took a dim view of Jewish accommodation to Hellenism.

1. Think of some changes in society you've recently observed. These could involve technology, sports, entertainment, or moral values. Try to be specific.

2. As you think about these changes, how have they affected you personally?

3. In what ways have these changes been positive, leading to better living and satisfaction with life? How have these changes been negative?

4. How do your respond to changes that have negative effects on you, your family, or your community? Try to be specific.

T W O

The Resistors

Luke 6:12–16 *In these days he went out to the mountain to pray; and all night he continued in prayer to God.* *[13]And when it was day, he called his disciples, and chose from them twelve, whom he named apostles;* *[14]Simon, whom he named Peter, and Andrew his brother, and James and John, and Philip, and Bartholomew,* *[15]and Matthew, and Thomas, and James the son of Alphaeus, and Simon who was called the Zealot,* *[16]and Judas the son of James, and Judas Iscariot, who became a traitor.*

Understanding the Word. The passage given above may seem to have no immediate connection with this week's lesson. In this scene, Luke names the twelve chosen to accompany Jesus in his journey and ministry. So what might have this to do with the context of the New Testament?

The thing possibly worth noting in this passage from Luke is that the second Simon is distinguished in verse 15 from the first Simon (Peter, verse 14). This second Simon is specifically identified as a *Zealot*.

This term is the subject of debate in New Testament scholarship, but it may suggest Simon's involvement with a party of like-minded Jews who vigorously opposed the advance of Hellenism. As such, they would have been direct opponents of the Sadducees and their accommodating tendencies. In some cases, they were militant, willing to fight Hellenistic sympathizers, even if they were fellow Jews. They often congregated in the wilderness, using remote areas to organize and attack like the revolutionaries of Judas Maccabeus's day.

In some cases, Zealots resorted to terrorist tactics. Hiding short, curved daggers (called *sicarii*) under their belts, militant Zealots would gather in crowded assemblies near prominent officials targeted by the party. In the midst of the throng, the dagger-carrying individual would slip the weapon out, thrust it into the victim, then withdraw quickly. Because of bodies pressed closely together, the perpetrator would be able to escape without notice.

We can't be sure whether Simon was a member of such a party or not, or if so, to what degree he was involved. Nor can we be absolutely certain that the Zealots were an organized party. In any case, we can be sure, based on the historical records of Josephus, that certain Jews were willing to take up arms in an effort to resist the advances of pagan Greek culture.

This serves to illustrate that Hellenism was not embraced by all Jews. It also may serve to illustrate that the ranks of Jesus' twelve disciples consisted of a rather motley crew.

1. How do you feel about the fact that one of Jesus' twelve disciples may have carried a concealed weapon?

2. Is it appropriate for followers of Jesus—then or now—to carry weapons?

3. When, if ever, is it acceptable for a Christian to make use of weapons as an exercise of force?

THREE

The Separatists

Mark 1:4–6 *John the baptizer appeared in the wilderness, preaching a baptism of repentance for the forgiveness of sins. ⁵And there went out to him all the country of Judea, and all the people of Jerusalem; and they were baptized by him in the* *river Jordan, confessing their sins. ⁶Now John was clothed with camel's hair, and had a leather girdle around his waist, and ate locusts and wild honey.*

Understanding the Word. You might be asking yourself, *Didn't we read this passage in the first week of lessons?* In fact, we did.

This time as we read, though, note the particularities about John. He hung out in the desert. His ministry was a ministry of preparation. He wore camel's hair and a leather belt. He dined on bugs and honey. Odd, don't you think?

In reality, several aspects of this description point to the possibility that John was a member of a separatist group. Some scholars even suggest that John was orphaned at an early age (recall that his parents were advanced in years; see Luke 1:7), and then raised by a separatist group. As with Simon the Zealot, we cannot be absolutely sure about John's affiliations, but several things do connect John with a group known as the Essenes. These were people who rejected Hellenism, but unlike the Zealots, they chose to retreat rather than resist. They established communities in remote places, the most famous of which was the settlement at Qumran on the northwest shore of the Dead Sea. This site has special significance because in 1947 a shepherd discovered a number of clay jars filled with ancient manuscripts. These manuscripts were remnants of a library maintained by the Essene community around the time of Jesus, and are known today as the Dead Sea Scrolls. These documents have not only changed the landscape of biblical scholarship by giving us an unprecedented view of the first-century context, they have also greatly bolstered our confidence in the reliability of the Old Testament as we have it today.

As a separatist movement, the Essenes awaited the coming judgment of God. In this regard, they represented the opposite extreme of the Sadducees' reliance upon human agency and free will. The Essenes had a far more deterministic or fatalistic worldview that surrendered all matters to God. Their primary purpose was to live holy lives until the day that the Lord would execute judgment upon the wicked and accommodating practices of the Jerusalem Jews.

The Essenes were also known for their daily bathings as a means of maintaining ritual purity. They lived by a strict code called "The Community Rule," and that rule spells out the terms for membering into the community. Some of those terms involved initiation, the abandonment of personal goods and wealth, and daily patterns of living. In some ways, these communities might be thought of as the forerunners of monasteries and convents.

Much about the picture we have of John suggests that he may have been—at least at one time—affiliated with the Essenes, although nothing in Scripture confirms that (in fact, the Essenes aren't even mentioned in the Bible). Nevertheless, this depiction does shed further light on the variety of responses to Hellenism's advance: while the Sadducees accommodated it and the Zealots resisted it, the Essenes withdrew from it.

1. As you read about the Essenes, what do you think of their solution? Is withdrawing from society an appropriate action?

2. Where do you see evidence of separatist groups today (i.e., groups that have withdrawn from society because of religious or political beliefs)?

3. Are you ever tempted to separate from society for social, political, or religious reasons? If so, what are those reasons? What would be the advantages of separating? What would be the consequences?

FOUR

Those in the World but Not of It

Mark 12:13–17 *And they sent to him some of the Pharisees and some of the Hero'di-ans, to entrap him in his talk.* [14]*And they came and said to him, "Teacher, we know that you are true, and care for no man; for you do not regard the position of men, but truly teach the way of God. Is it lawful to pay taxes to Caesar, or not?* [15]*Should we pay them, or should we not?" But knowing their hypocrisy, he said to them, "Why put me to the test? Bring me a coin, and let me look at it."* [16]*And they brought one. And he said to them, "Whose likeness and inscription is this?" They said to him, "Caesar's." * [17]*Jesus said to them, "Render to Caesar the things that are Caesar's, and to God the things that are God's." And they were amazed at him.*

Understanding the Word. So far we've seen at least three possible responses to Hellenism in the first century: accommodation, resistance, and separation. It seems that at some level there is a problem with each of the three, for none really seems to be in a position to engage the surrounding culture for change without being consumed by it.

In Week 6 we discussed the party of the Pharisees, too often known simply as hypocrites. Of the various responses to pagan influences, the Pharisees were the one organized group who resolved to be in the world but not of it. Theirs was a delicate balance between assimilation and isolation. They strove to pursue God's holiness through everyday life in the midst of a surrounding culture gone wrong. But it's a dangerous position to maintain when one tries to maintain close contact with the culture without being drawn into it.

I'm told that lifeguards and rescue swimmers are often trained to push away from victims in distress. Why might this be the case? Oftentimes, and because of panic, drowning victims will grab on to their rescuers and inadvertently drag the rescuers down with them. When dealing with victims who won't respond to instructions, rescue swimmers are trained to plant their feet firmly in victims' chests and strongly push them away. Yet the rescuer never gets more than an arm's length away from the victim.

In our passage today, the Pharisees who have assembled to test Jesus may well have represented a splinter group of the larger party, for one can hardly imagine a Pharisee who would conspire with Herodians. The Herodians were likely members of the royal court of Herod, and as such would have fully supported Hellenistic ideas. Perhaps because Jesus was a common threat to both the Pharisees and the Herodians, we see an unlikely and unholy alliance.

Once again, the Pharisees (at least those present in this scene) fail to distinguish between the inner and outer aspects of matters. Their question concerns the practice of taxpaying. They seem incapable of delving more deeply into the foundational issue at hand.

1. In what ways do you strive to be holy in this world? How does your pursuit of personal holiness distinguish you from those around you who are living according to worldly standards?

2. In what ways are you living as one of this world? How does living by worldly standards affect your witness and testimony to others? Try to think of specific practices you regularly or occasionally engage in.

3. How can you do a better job of living in the world without being of it? Again, try to think in specific, concrete terms.

FIVE

The Followers

Mark 12:28–34 *And one of the scribes came up and heard them disputing with one another, and seeing that he answered them well, asked him, "Which commandment is the first of all?" [29]Jesus answered, "The first is, 'Hear, O Israel: The Lord our God, the Lord is one; [30]and you shall love the Lord your God with all your heart, and with all your soul, and with all your mind, and with all your strength.' [31]The second is this, 'You shall love your neighbor as yourself.' There is no other commandment greater than these." [32]And the scribe said to him, "You are right, Teacher; you have truly said that he is one, and there is no other but he; [33]and to love him with all the heart, and with all the understanding, and with all the strength, and to love one's neighbor as oneself, is much more than all whole burnt offerings and sacrifices." [34]And when Jesus saw that he answered wisely, he said to him, "You are not far from the kingdom of God." And after that no one dared to ask him any question.*

Understanding the Word. When the Jews returned from Babylon to resettle their homeland in and around Jerusalem, they returned with a new commitment to keeping God's law. As we saw in Week 6, the religious leaders developed a set of oral laws designed to function as a hedge of protection around the written law. The thinking was this: "if we don't break the oral law, there's no chance of breaking the written law." (Recall my earlier illustration of how I create a hedge of protection around my Pepsi.)

Out of this circumstance emerged a new role among Judaism: the scribe. As we saw earlier in our study, these folks are too often simply thought of as secretaries or clerks. In reality, they were likely the professional scholars of the day, the local experts on religious matters. They are often brought to bear in scenes where religious questions are raised.

What's interesting to me about this passage is that it comes on the heels of two other challenges levied against Jesus by religious leaders. The first was by the Pharisees (and the Herodians) in connection to taxation. The second was by the Sadducees to marriage. In each case, Jesus turns the tables on his would-be detractors, sending them away with their tails between their legs.

In the third case, however, a religious scholar approaches him (not surprisingly) with a question about the law. In his asking, one gets the sense that his pursuit was not to trick or trap Jesus, but to gain a fuller understanding. When the scribe accepts Jesus' response as true, Jesus commends the man.

This demonstrates how complex human dynamics can be. We saw earlier how some Pharisees were in cooperation with Herodians, which would normally have been unthinkable. This highlights potential divisions within the party. Likewise, we observe a similar division:

> They brought to the Pharisees the man who had formerly been blind. Now it was a sabbath day when Jesus made the clay and opened his eyes. The Pharisees again asked him how he had received his sight. And he said to them, "He put clay on my eyes, and I washed, and I see." Some of the Pharisees said, "This man is not from God, for he does not keep the sabbath." But others said, "How can a man who is a sinner do such signs?" There was a division among them. (John 9:13–16)

Perhaps one lesson to be learned from the reading this week is this: while one can certainly maintain affiliations with and allegiances to organized groups (like religious denominations, political parties, or even fan clubs), one must never let those affiliations and allegiances cloud one's thinking. In this week's reading, we see how certain Pharisees, Herodians, and Sadducees were overly committed to their own party line, so much so that they could not allow their minds to embrace the truth of Jesus' teaching. The scribe, however, is exemplary insofar as he refuses to let his own ties—or even his own social standing—interfere with his reception of the right teaching of Jesus.

1. The scribe in today's lesson was willing to step out from the party line of the religious establishment. How does Mark portray his decision: favorably or unfavorably?

2. Where in life do you find yourself going against the party line of your school, company, or organization?

3. How could you as a Christian attempt to bring about change or reform to your school, company, or organization without being seen as hostile or divisive?

COMMENTARY NOTES

Day 1. The word *apocrypha* comes from a Greek word meaning "hidden" or "obscure." It has come to refer to a set of books included in the Roman Catholic Bible but not the Protestant Bible. Whereas the Protestant Bible contains sixty-six books (thirty-nine in the Old Testament and twenty-seven in the New Testament), the Roman Catholic Bible contains seventy-three books. The Protestant term for this set of books is the Apocrypha; Roman Catholics refer to these books as "deuterocanonical," meaning "second canon." By this Roman Catholics mean that this set of books holds a place in the Bible alongside the other sixty-six books as authoritative over matters of doctrine and practice.

The seven books disputed by Protestants have unique features. First, they were likely written after the Old Testament documents. Some of the books address circumstances taking place between the time periods of the Old and New Testaments (a time known as the Intertestamental period from roughly 450 BC until the time of Christ). Unlike the rest of the Old Testament, which was originally written in Hebrew (and some Aramaic), the seven additional books of the Roman Catholic Bible were originally written in Greek. It wasn't until the Old Testament—or Hebrew Bible—was translated from its original languages into Greek that the extra books were included with it.

Although Protestants do not treat the Apocrypha as having the same inspired authority as the sixty-six books of their Bible, they nevertheless appreciate the enormous value the books of the Apocrypha lend to our study of the Bible. One important contribution of the Apocrypha is its provision of key historical information that gives shape to our understanding of the events and context of the New Testament.

Day 2. Judas Maccabeus (meaning "hammer") led a Jewish revolution to reclaim Jerusalem and its temple from Syrian occupation. In 164 BC, he successfully rededicated the temple on December 25. The ongoing festival that commemorates this act is known as Hanukkah. Judas Maccabeus eventually ruled over Israel, establishing a dynasty in his family name of the Hasmoneans. His rule is recorded in part in the apocryphal books of 1–4 Maccabees.

Day 3. Determinism and fatalism are close related philosophies that hold to divine control over all affairs. Since God is assumed to have predetermined the outcome of human choices and actions, all matters are attributable to him and there is essentially no place for free will or human agency.

Day 5. Mark gives a richer description of the scribes in 12:38. Here, he writes, "And in his teaching [Jesus] said, 'Beware of the scribes, who like to go about in long robes, and to have salutations in the market places and the best seats in the synagogues and the places of honor at feasts, who devour widows' houses and for a pretense make long prayers. They will receive the greater condemnation.'"

Again, it is important to remember that not all members of a community or organization such as the scribes operated in exactly the same ways.

WEEK NINE

GATHERING DISCUSSION OUTLINE

A. Open session in prayer. Ask for specific celebrations of God's goodness.

B. What new insights have you gained from this week's readings? What has encouraged you? What has challenged you?

C. View video for this week's readings.

D. Discuss questions selected from daily readings.

1. **KEY OBSERVATION:** The Sadducees embraced the world around them.

DISCUSSION QUESTION: Think about your church or your denomination. How has it embraced worldly practices?

2. **KEY OBSERVATION:** The Zealots fought against the world around them.

DISCUSSION QUESTION: At what point is fighting against the world justifiable for Christians? (This could lead to a heated discussion. Please be considerate of all opinions; the aim here is to consider, not resolve.)

3. **KEY OBSERVATION:** The Essenes withdrew from the world around them.

DISCUSSION QUESTION: At what point is separation justified for Christians? Where do you see evidence that this can be a fruitful, God-honoring move? How can it be problematic?

4. **KEY OBSERVATION:** The Pharisees tried to live in the world but not of it.

   DISCUSSION QUESTION: Is it really possible to be in the world yet not be of it? How do you feel about the Pharisees' attempt to do so? What lessons can Christians today learn from their solution?

5. **KEY OBSERVATION:** God calls us to be a holy people, set apart from the world we live in.

   DISCUSSION QUESTION: When you think of the word *holiness*, what images does your mind conjure up? Are those images positive or negative? Discuss in your group possible ways that holiness could become a compelling alternative to those living according to worldly standards.

E. What facts and information presented in the commentary portion of the lesson help you understand the weekly Scripture?

F. Close session with prayer. Ask for specific concerns to be brought before our Lord.

WEEK TEN

Mark 12:41–13:37

The Eschaton

INTRODUCTION

At this point in our journey through Mark, it may be helpful to review where we've been. In his prologue, Mark begins in the middle of things. His opening unit gives us the background information we need to make sense of his story within the context of a larger narrative we often call salvation history (Week 1). From there, we see that Jesus' ministry is aimed at turning an upside-down world right-side up. Every effort by Jesus to restore persons to fruitful living confirms his commitment to bringing the world back into the shape for which it was created in the beginning. Toward this end, Jesus comes preaching with authority, casting out demons, healing the sick, and forgiving sins (Week 2). As his fame spreads, the religious establishment becomes increasingly uncomfortable with his teachings, especially his claim to authority over sin. Jesus is fully aware of their murmurings against him and teaches a series of lessons through word pictures highlighting their inability to think outside the box. Contrary to their opinion, Jesus demonstrates that God's grace is far bigger than they are willing to imagine (Week 3).

Using more word pictures through parables, Jesus compares people to various types of soils, only some of which receive the Word of God and cultivate a climate conducive for that seed to grow (Week 4). Like unproductive soils, some people are hardened by fear, shame, or anger—each force working in direct opposition to fruitful living. Fruitful living requires faith, here understood as active trust (Week 5). Ironically, the Pharisees—as experts in religious matters—are the least likely to understand this. Their insistent adherence to their traditions fuels a fire of fear that, like a virus, spreads uncontrollably (Week 6).

Near the center of Mark's Gospel, we find a very dark twist to the plot: Jesus announces that his purpose for coming into the world is to be a ransom for many. He is, as the Christ, anointed to die. Peter cannot and will not accept this reality. Perhaps as a sign of assurance from God, Jesus is transfigured before their very eyes and gives some of his disciples—including Peter—a vision of his future glory (Week 7).

True to his mission, Jesus journeys toward Jerusalem and the site of his eventual execution. He takes the occasion to offer another parable in which the religious leaders are likened to wicked tenants in charge of a vineyard who refuse to give the absent landowner his share and abuse or murder those sent to collect that share (Week 8). And true to his prediction, the religious establishment becomes bolder in their attempts to stop Jesus' message and ministry. In turn, at least two of the religious factions attempt to discredit him, but to no avail (Week 9). Thus, the stage is set for Jesus' final days.

ONE

Injustice

Mark 12:41–44 *And he sat down opposite the treasury, and watched the multitude putting money into the treasury. Many rich people put in large sums. ⁴²And a poor widow came, and put in two copper coins, which make a penny. ⁴³And he called his disciples to him, and said to them, "Truly, I say to you, this poor widow has put in more than all those who are contributing to the treasury. ⁴⁴For they all contributed out of their abundance; but she out of her poverty has put in everything she had, her whole living."*

Understanding the Word. As with so many of Mark's scenes, this one can only really be understood within context.

In the preceding scenes, Jesus receives challenges from Pharisees and Sadducees. After turning the tables on them, Jesus is then approached by a scribe who asks what seems to be a sincere question. In fact, Jesus says to the scribe, "You are not far from the kingdom of God" (12:34). Truly, this scribe is an exception to the typical pattern of scribes, for on the heels of this encounter, Jesus says to the crowds assembled around him,

> Beware of the scribes, who like to go about in long robes, and to have salutations in the market places and the best seats in the synagogues and the places of honor at feasts, who devour widows' houses and for a pretense make long prayers. They will receive the greater condemnation. (Mark 12:38–40)

Of particular note here is Jesus' reference to the scribes' practice of devouring widows' houses. It is probably not mere coincidence that Jesus tells the story of the widow's offering in his very next breath; rather, Jesus seems to be drawing a direct correlation between scribal social practices and the widow's poverty.

This highlights an important theme in Mark's Gospel: social injustice. Recall that Jesus takes an earlier stab at unjust practices in Mark 7:

> You [the Pharisees and scribes] say, "If a man tells his father or his mother, What you would have gained from me is Corban" (that is, given to God)— then you no longer permit him to do anything for his father or mother, thus making void the word of God through your tradition which you hand on. And many such things you do. (vv. 11–13)

It would appear that the religious leaders who had been established as stewards over God's people were instead lording their position over the people. This took place in part through their self-serving practices and policies. Jesus is quick to note in his parable of the wicked tenants that the religious leaders maintained impure motives, going so far as killing the landowner's son in order to capture the assets of the landowner: "This is the heir; come, let us kill him, and the inheritance will be ours" (12:7).

The story of the widow and her meager but sacrificial offering serves as a foil in the story by highlighting her remarkable faithfulness against the greed and corruption of the religious establishment. Similarly, the story of the inquiring scribe in the preceding passage serves as a foil to the typical religious leaders who seek to destroy Jesus rather than to gain the wisdom he has to offer. Mark, as an inspired writer, is capturing these important contrasts that Jesus creates in his public dealings with the Jerusalem crowd. The people of God have been and remain under oppression—not just by Rome, but ironically by God's would-be representatives on earth. The time has come for justice to be served—a time when God "will come and destroy the tenants, and give the vineyard to others" (12:9).

It is a time of oppression and social injustice indeed; but it is also a time pregnant with hope and expectancy.

1. How would you characterize your giving to your local church: as sacrificial (like the widow) or as convenient (like the rich people)?

2. What prevents you—if anything—from giving extravagantly, even sacrificially, to your local church?

3. In what ways does withholding from the offering plate contribute to social and economic injustice within a congregation and community?

TWO

Apocalypse

Mark 13:26–29 *And then they will see the Son of man coming in clouds with great power and glory. ²⁷And then he will send out the angels, and gather his elect from the four winds, from the ends of the earth to the ends of heaven.*

²⁸"From the fig tree learn its lesson: as soon as its branch becomes tender and puts forth its leaves, you know that summer is near. ²⁹So also, when you see these things taking place, you know that he is near, at the very gates."

Understanding the Word. Chapter 13 in Mark is often referred to as "The Little Apocalypse," largely because it bears the same stamp of apocalyptic, otherworldly emphasis that the book of Revelation does.

Coming from the Greek word *apokalyptō* (meaning "to make visible or known; to reveal"; compare the term *apocrypha* from last week's lesson), the English word *apocalypse* typically carries with it images of future judgment, the end of the world, trials and tribulations, and cosmic battle . . . and for good reason. The book of Revelation (the "Apocalypse") is so named because of the type of literature it represents: a look at future events in light of the ultimate judgment of the earth by God. Revelation isn't the only place in the Bible where we find this type of literature. We see it in the books of Daniel and Ezekiel. We see it here in Mark. We also see it outside the Bible in what is called the *pseudepigrapha*, or "false writings." These are religious writings for sure, but not authoritatively embraced by the traditions of orthodox Christianity (or orthodox Judaism).

What is apocalyptic literature? Although there is no set definition, there are a variety of features that tend to be common to these kinds of writings. For one thing, apocalyptic literature tends to be very graphic. It features rich imagery and symbolism. For another, it often involves a visionary experience, and sometimes the mediation of an angel or angelic messenger who guides the one having the vision.

Apocalyptic literature often deals with the final and culminating days of the cosmos, or the *eschaton*. But perhaps no single feature is more evident across all types of apocalyptic literature than the emphasis on divine judgment, the condemnation of the wicked, and the vindication of the righteous. This feature stands out clearly in the passage for today's reading, and reveals one of the primary purposes of apocalyptic literature: to encourage people under persecution.

God's people are no strangers to persecution. Scripture recounts numerous instances of Jews and Christians being persecuted—sometimes horribly—for their faith in the one true God. In the New Testament period, the beheading of John (Mark 6), the crucifixion of Jesus (Mark 15), and the stoning of Stephen (Acts 7) all attest to Roman and Jewish opposition to followers of the Way. That Peter denied Jesus three times reveals that the threat against followers of Jesus was real. Even Paul, before his Damascus Road conversion in Acts 9, was part of a systematic persecution of the early church.

Eventually, opposition to Christianity reached Rome, and Christians began to be persecuted in ways previously unimagined. The Roman emperor Nero is said to have lit the streets of Rome with burning bodies of Christians. Amid such atrocities, God's people needed solid reminders that their God was still in control. Apocalyptic literature provided that assurance.

1. Revelation is the most well-known example of apocalyptic literature in the Bible. When you think of the book of Revelation, what images and thoughts come to mind?

2. What, if anything, in today's world serves a similar function as apocalyptic literature? Can you think of any counterparts?

3. When you read apocalyptic works like Revelation and Mark 13, do you find yourself reading in fear or in hope? Do these works scare you, or do they encourage you?

THREE

The Destruction of Jerusalem

Mark 13:1–2 *And as he came out of the temple, one of his disciples said to him, "Look, Teacher, what wonderful stones and what wonderful buildings!" ²And Jesus said to him, "Do you see these great buildings? There will not be left here one stone upon another, that will not be thrown down."*

Understanding the Word. One of the things that is remarkably overlooked in today's sermons is any discussion of the destruction of Jerusalem in AD 70, and its role in the New Testament. The background to this event consists of a series of Jewish uprisings and resistance efforts against Roman occupation of the Jewish region. Various individuals arose, sometimes claiming to be the Messiah. To many, the Messiah would be a political leader who would restore Israel by military means to its former prominence. Since Jesus did not emerge as that kind of Messiah, many were disillusioned with him and sought other means to accomplish their political and military aims.

In today's passage, Jesus makes a rather mysterious comment about the future of the grand buildings of Jerusalem. The disciples seem to understand that Jesus is pointing to an eventual destruction of the city of some sort, but they don't know when. Without giving any exact times, Jesus assures them that, "Truly, I say to you, this generation will not pass away before all these things take place" (13:30).

The first-century Jewish historian, Josephus, gives us remarkable commentary on the events leading up to the destruction of the city in AD 70. Prior to that, and as mentioned above, Jews began to protest Roman occupation of Palestine. Rome sent a military battalion under the leadership of Vespasian to suppress the revolt. Jewish rebels sealed off the city, and used it as a fortress. Within the city, rations of food and provisions ran in short supply as Rome laid siege to the city month after month and year after year. As conditions worsened and people began to starve, factions within the city began to war with one another in pursuit of their dwindling resources. Circumstances became dire. One account describes how a mother ate her newborn child.

Outside the city, Rome employed various siege works in an effort to break down the defenses of the city. The effort was long and sustained, and the Roman army eventually penetrated the walls of the city, setting fire to the temple and destroying virtually everything in sight. Judaism as it had been known for centuries was no more. Although it is debatable what direct effect this event had on the early Christians, Judaism at that time was forever impacted by the loss of the temple. Most scholars feel that the Pharisees were the only Jewish sect to survive, as Judaism became a religion increasingly centered on Scripture when sacrifices could no longer be made at the temple.

Some New Testament scholars believe that the Gospels may have been written after the destruction of the temple. This position is difficult to maintain, however, since such an extraordinary event would certainly have been included in the Gospel writers' accounts, especially in view of Jesus' unthinkable prediction forty years earlier that the temple would fall. Other scholars believe the Gospels were written in close proximity to these events. This seems more likely, especially with respect to Matthew and Luke. Regardless, the historical realities of the event confirm Jesus' prophecy about the temple structure. And as we will see in the next lesson, even some of the more outlandish prophecies given by Jesus have confirmation outside the New Testament.

1. What did you know of the destruction of Jerusalem in AD 70 prior to this study?

2. How might this knowledge be important for understanding this week's passage?

3. Of what benefit would this information be if it were made available to local churches through pulpit preaching, Bible studies, Sunday schools, and small group lessons?

4. What might you do to encourage others to delve into biblical and church history a bit deeper?

FOUR

Signs and Portents

Mark 13:24–25 *"But in those days, after that tribulation, the sun will be darkened, and the moon will not give its light, [25]and the stars will be falling from heaven, and the powers in the heavens will be shaken."*

Understanding the Word. In yesterday's lesson, we considered the importance of knowing the history of the time period surrounding Jesus' life, especially as we examine Jesus' prophecies in Mark 13. In addition to the fulfillment of Jesus' prediction that Jerusalem's temple would be destroyed, Jesus also predicted another number of supernatural phenomena. (A quick review of the whole of Mark 13 will be helpful if time permits.)

I must say from the outset of this lesson that our faith does not require absolute proof or evidence. If it did, faith would no longer be faith, but sight. As the apostle Paul says in 2 Corinthians 5:7, "We walk by faith, not by sight." Nevertheless, our faith is a reasoned faith arising from historical persons accomplishing acts in real time and in real places. It is good news for us that the historical evidence increasingly confirms the truth claims of the Bible.

We have already mentioned at a number of points the first-century Jewish historian, Josephus. In his chronicles of the fall of Jerusalem to Rome, he notes a number of supernatural phenomena that preceded the final days before the city's collapse. What is remarkable is the degree to which some of his reports parallel Jesus' predictions forty years earlier. You will recall that Jesus said, "False Christs and false prophets will arise and show signs and wonders, to lead astray, if possible, the elect" (Mark 13:22). Josephus tells us that many false prophets arose and deceived the people (*Wars* 5:286). Jesus predicted that, "the stars will be falling from heaven" (Mark 13:25). Josephus reports that a star appeared over Jerusalem resembling a sword and a comet remained over the city for an entire year (*Wars* 5:289).

Jesus went on to say that, "they will see the Son of man coming in clouds with great power and glory. And then he will send out the angels . . ." (Mark 13:26–27), whereas Josephus tells us that chariots and troops of armored soldiers were seen running among the clouds (*Wars* 5:298–299). According to Jesus, the angels would "gather his elect from the four winds, from the ends of the earth to the ends of heaven" (Mark 13:27). Josephus tells of a man who began to cry in the streets, "A voice from the east, a voice from the west, a voice from the four winds, a voice against Jerusalem and the holy house" (*Wars* 5:301).

As one reads through Josephus's accounts, it's hard not to be struck by the correspondence of Jesus' predictions with Josephus's historical reports. However, and at this point, I need to state clearly that I am *in no way* suggesting that the reports of Josephus absolutely confirm Jesus' predictions beyond a reasonable shadow of doubt. What I *am* suggesting is that Josephus provides an amazingly detailed account of supernatural phenomena that seem to broadly align with Jesus' prophecies in Mark 13, and within the time frame Jesus suggested (namely, a generation or so; see 13:30). My point is this: our faith is a reasoned faith, and appeals to historical evidence like the writings of Josephus—who was not a Christian, nor was he vested in the Christian enterprise—only heighten my confidence in the truthfulness of Scripture and the claims it makes.

1. What strikes you most about today's lesson? Do you find the possible connections between Jesus' prophecy and Josephus's reports to be of interest, or do these possible connections seem far-fetched?

2. Would you like to know more about Josephus and his historical writings? (The standard book for Josephus is *The Works of Josephus: Complete and Unabridged*, translated by William Whiston from which references in today's lesson come. You can also consult a number of online, free-access versions of Josephus's writings.)

3. Perhaps spend a few minutes today doing a bit of online research about Josephus. A good starting point is his short autobiography, commonly known as *The Life of Flavius Josephus*.

FIVE

No One Knows

Mark 13:3–4, 32–33 *And as he sat on the Mount of Olives opposite the temple, Peter and James and John and Andrew asked him privately, *[4]*"Tell us,* *when will this be, and what will be the sign when these things are all to be accomplished?" . . .*

[32]"But of that day or that hour no one knows, not even the angels in heaven, nor the Son, but only the Father. [33]Take heed, watch; for you do not know when the time will come.

Understanding the Word. Growing up in the 1970s and '80s, the end of the world was regularly on my mind. It was the era of the Cold War between the USSR and the United States. Nuclear holocaust was a pervasive concern. Thoughts of the end occupied our attention in the news, at the cinema, and in our literature. I recall reading George Orwell's *1984* as a freshman in high school, just five years before the dreaded date. The threat of Big Brother loomed large even though 1984 seemed a long way off at the time.

I also recall the television network broadcast of a made-for-TV movie called *The Day After*. The plot involved a full-scale nuclear exchange between the US and the Soviet Union. The movie was heavily publicized, and the viewing audience did not disappoint: it remains among the highest-rated (if not *the* highest-rated) television movies of all time. On the campus of Purdue University, my buddies and I waited with untold millions across the country for the airing of this momentous film. When the ABC special feature aired, all eyes were on the TV. I remember going down the hallway of Tarkington Hall to the bathroom during a commercial break. The dorm was dead silent, and not a soul in sight. All were huddled in dorm rooms around small televisions.

As an undergraduate, I even remember taking a course that offered a module on nuclear holocaust. As with a train wreck, I simply could not divert my attention from the threat of an imminent end. Fueling the fire was a book by Hal Lindsey entitled *The Late Great Planet Earth* in which Lindsey brought together current events and biblical prophecies, concluding that the end of the world was at hand.

Add to that the prognostications of Nostradamus, cult episodes like those of Jim Jones and David Koresh, and the massively popular Left Behind series, and we have the makings for a full-blown apocalyptic crisis.

In Jesus' day, the threat was different, but no less real. Messianic pretenders abounded before, during, and after the life of Jesus. In each case, they claimed to be the one chosen to restore Israel. In a real sense, these pretenders functioned as *Antichrists*. To be sure, the people of Jesus' day likewise had concerns about an upheaval of their present order.

Jesus sets out to lay all those fears to rest. He assures us that no one, not even he, knows when all these things will happen: "But of that day or that hour no one knows, not even the angels in heaven, nor the Son, but only the Father. Take heed, watch; for you do not know when the time will come" (Mark 13:32–33).

Instead of worrying about, or calculating, or predicting when and where the end will come, Jesus admonishes his hearers to remain faithful, trusting that God will send his Spirit to encourage and equip his followers on that day.

1. Attempts are often made to accurately determine when the end will come. What are some of the attempts you recall hearing?

2. As you think about efforts to predict the end, how would you describe the sources of these efforts? Said differently, what kinds of groups or individuals are most likely to make such predictions?

3. Why do you suppose God would withhold the knowledge of the end from everyone in the world, including Jesus? Really think about this one for a moment.

4. How would you live your life differently if you knew: (a) when the end would come; and (b) that the end would occur within your lifetime?

COMMENTARY NOTES

General Comments. The term *eschaton* comes from a Greek word meaning "last" or "final." In its noun form as used in this lesson, it refers to the end times. The study of the end times is a discipline called *eschatology*.

Day 2. The phrase "let the reader understand" in 13:14 has generated a good deal of discussion among scholars. On one hand, "the reader" could refer to the one who is reading Mark's Gospel to him- or herself. On the other hand, it could refer to a public reader of the text. In the days of Mark, a very small percentage of the population was literate. The typical way to "read" a written work like Mark's Gospel was to hear it read aloud. Mark's statement may have been directed to such a public reader; even if so, it is not immediately clear how this cue would function.

Another perplexing question is whether or not these were Jesus' words uttered as he spoke, or whether this is Mark's insertion as a parenthetical comment. You may recall from Week 6 that Mark uses such insertions from time to time to clarify or explain. Regardless of one's views, this statement remains something of a mystery, which is not surprising given that Mark wrote nearly two thousand years ago in a language and on land very foreign to us.

Day 3. In ancient times, cities were often built on summits so that they could be more easily defended. Jerusalem is no exception. As with other cities of that time, Jerusalem was fortified with very strong walls to make it even more difficult for advancing armies to enter the city. When Roman forces came to suppress the Jewish rebellion in Jerusalem, they came with heavy equipment designed to build ramps up the side of the mountain so that offensive weapons like battering rams could be positioned to attack the walls of the city. The effort would be a massive engineering undertaking and would take months, if not years, to accomplish.

At the same time, the Roman forces would have created a blockade at the foot of the summit, making it difficult if not impossible for people within the walls to obtain provisions. The Roman government would certainly hope that the holdouts would peacefully abandon their positions due to starvation so that Rome could avoid the cost (in material and personnel) of warfare.

These are typical features of laying siege to a city, and the instruments of such warfare are called *siege works*.

Day 5. Even before the time of Jesus, some claimed to be the long-awaited Messiah. For example, a certain Judas of Galilee led an uprising against Roman authority in response to a census imposed by Rome for purposes of taxation. This took place in the year AD 6. His efforts were brutally crushed by Roman forces. Others followed through the first century. These individuals are called *messianic pretenders*. They are also referred to as *Antichrists*.

WEEK TEN

GATHERING DISCUSSION OUTLINE

A. Open session in prayer. Ask for specific celebrations of God's goodness.

B. What new insights have you gained from this week's readings? What has encouraged you? What has challenged you?

C. View video for this week's readings.

D. Discuss questions selected from daily readings.

1. **KEY OBSERVATION:** Jesus' entry to Jerusalem came at a time when injustice was rampant.

   DISCUSSION QUESTION: It may seem surprising that some of the injustice experienced by poor people in Jerusalem was actually being committed by the religious establishment. In what ways might our own church practices and policies create a similar circumstance for poor people today?

2. **KEY OBSERVATION:** Apocalyptic literature encourages readers to be sure that God will punish the wicked and reward the righteous.

   DISCUSSION QUESTION: What role, if any, does apocalyptic literature play in our lives today? How important is it to know how things end and that good will triumph over evil? Try to be specific in your responses.

3. **KEY OBSERVATION:** Jesus predicted the destruction of Jerusalem forty years before it actually happened.

DISCUSSION QUESTION: What is the role between faith and evidence? How important should evidence be to our faith? Read Hebrews 11:1 and discuss this passage in light of this week's reading and the role of historical evidence.

4. **KEY OBSERVATION:** Some of the supernatural phenomena that Jesus predicted may have connections to Josephus's reports of signs and portents just prior to the fall of Jerusalem.

   DISCUSSION QUESTION: Does the account of Josephus impact your view of Jesus' prophecy in any way? Why or why not?

5. **KEY OBSERVATION:** No one knows when the end will come.

   DISCUSSION QUESTION: How does our knowledge of the end shape our lives and the way we live them today?

E. What facts and information presented in the commentary portion of the lesson help you understand the weekly Scripture?

F. Close session with prayer. Ask for specific concerns to be brought before our Lord.

WEEK ELEVEN

Mark 14:1–72

Betrayed

INTRODUCTION

You may not have noticed, but the pace of Mark's narrative is slowing down. It is commonly held that Jesus' ministry lasted about three years. Mark's account of the life of Jesus focuses on Jesus' public life: his teaching, miracles, and death. Except for the brief period of John the Baptizer's preparatory ministry, all of Mark takes place within the span of these three years, and the vast majority of that time is covered within the first ten chapters of Mark.

Chapter 11 of Mark begins a change in pace. With Jesus' entry into Jerusalem, Mark gives increasing attention to the details of the last week of Jesus' life. Events become accentuated, and at times, Mark cuts away from the main action involving Jesus to include parallel narration of things like Judas's betrayal and Peter's denial of Jesus. The last week of Jesus' life (the "Passion") occupies a large focus in Mark . . . nearly half of his Gospel, in fact. It has been said about Mark that it is essentially a Passion narrative with a very long introduction.

Knowing this helps us appreciate the degree to which Mark is giving primary attention to what he deems most important: the Jerusalem events of the last week of Jesus' life. Those events really come into focus as we move into the final chapters of Mark (14:1–16:6).

Consider all that happens in chapter 14 alone:

- The chief priests and scribes plot to seize Jesus
- A woman anoints Jesus with expensive oil
- Judas contracts with chief priests to hand over Jesus
- Jesus' disciples make preparations for the Passover meal

- Jesus and his disciples sit for the meal, during which time Jesus announces that he will be betrayed
- Jesus transforms the Passover meal into the Lord's Supper
- The group goes to Gethsemane for Jesus to pray
- Jesus is arrested and appears before the Sanhedrin
- Peter denies Jesus three times

Whew, that's a lot of activity.

ONE
Communion and Betrayal

Mark 14:1–2 *It was now two days before the Passover and the feast of Unleavened Bread. And the chief priests and the scribes were seeking how to arrest him by stealth, and kill him;* *²for they said, "Not during the feast, lest there be a tumult of the people."*

Understanding the Word. As we launch into chapter 14, two dominant themes emerge: *communion* and *betrayal*. The two verses for today bring these two themes into sharp contrast. By *communion* I mean fellowship, community, and relationship, especially as those are experienced in Mark's culture around the supper table. By *betrayal* I mean the exact opposite: *broken* fellowship, *broken* community, and *broken* relationship.

Here's an interesting exercise: note how many times Mark references something in regard to either communion (including table fellowship) or betrayal. In chapter 14, the number of such mentions is impressive. You might want to make a list of such words and the frequency with which they occur. A quick (and incomplete) glance reveals something like this:

Communion words and phrases: feast, bread, sat at table, Passover lamb, eat, drink, cup, etc.

Betrayal words and phrases: arrest, kill, betray, fall away, deny, seize, forsake, condemn, etc.

Like I said, the range and frequency of these words and phrases is noteworthy. In fact, they give chapter 14 a distinctive flavor. Further, the way Mark has arranged his narrative is also noteworthy. Take a moment and read through the whole chapter, specifically observing the alternating pattern of the paragraphs. Some are largely focused on communion, and have a more positive sense to them. Consider, for instance, the opening verses where the religious leaders are hampered in their efforts to apprehend Jesus because he is wildly popular with the crowd. The scene shifts immediately to a setting that confirms that Jesus is in Bethany, at the *house* of a *leper, eating* with a *leper!* The disciples are there, and an unnamed woman is there. We aren't sure who else was there, but it may have been a throng of people. It's a pretty happy scene.

Right on the heels of this scene, though, the story darkens when Judas slips away to accept a bounty contract for Jesus' life. From that point, the scenes keep alternating between scenes of fellowship and scenes of broken fellowship.

Further, there is something of a transition to the chapter. Whereas it opens with Jesus in good standing with the crowds and his disciples, you might notice how a gradual but definitive shift has taken place by the end of the chapter. Mark is up to something in the way that he is presenting his material. Our job as good readers is to pick up on these clues.

1. How distinctive is chapter 14 in terms of its emphasis on *communion* and *betrayal*? Are these categories that have been imposed onto the text, or does a close reading of the text lead you to this conclusion?

2. How sharp is the contrast between scenes? Again, is the contrast imposed, or is it fairly self-evident?

3. In what ways does the beginning of the chapter differ in tone from the end? What might Mark be suggesting to us about following Jesus through his structuring of the chapter in this way?

TWO

Costly Oil

Mark 14:3–9 *And while he was at Bethany in the house of Simon the leper, as he sat at table, a woman came with an alabaster flask of ointment of pure nard, very costly, and she broke the flask and poured it over his head. [4]But there were some who said to themselves indignantly, "Why was the ointment thus wasted?*

⁵For this ointment might have been sold for more than three hundred denarii, and given to the poor." And they reproached her. ⁶But Jesus said, "Let her alone; why do you trouble her? She has done a beautiful thing to me. ⁷For you always have the poor with you, and whenever you will, you can do good to them; but you will not always have me. ⁸She has done what she could; she has anointed my body beforehand for burying. ⁹And truly, I say to you, wherever the gospel is preached in the whole world, what she has done will be told in memory of her."

Understanding the Word. One of my favorite Bible stories is the contest between Elijah and the prophets of Baal on Mount Carmel in 1 Kings 18. If you've never read it, you may want to do so. After thoroughly disgracing those prophets, Elijah withdraws only to incur the wrath of the evil queen, Jezebel, whose hapless prophets are slaughtered by Elijah. When he learns that Jezebel has determined to kill him, he asks God to take his life. Dejected and despondent, Elijah senses that all hope for the redemption of God's people is lost, as he alone is the only remaining prophet for the one true God.

He withdraws further into the wilderness. While there, a tumultuous wind sweeps over the mountain, shattering stones. The wind is followed by a violent earthquake, and the earthquake by a consuming fire. In none of these calamities, however, does Elijah hear the voice of God. After all settles, the word of the Lord comes to him as a still, small voice that encourages Elijah and announces to him that there are others—indeed, lots of others—who still bear allegiance to the one true King.

Elijah's orders are straightforward: with his prophetic authority he is to appoint a new king over Syria, a new king over Israel, and a new prophet to succeed himself. The mission of God will move forward. In each case, the word used to define the appointment is the same word used to describe the woman's act of pouring costly fragrance over the head of Jesus: *anoint*.

We've already considered this word in Week 7. In fact, any treatment of Mark needs to give this word significant attention. It figures prominently in the major thought stream of Mark's Gospel.

The Hebrew word that gives us *Messiah* and the Greek word that gives us *Christ* both point to the same reality: to appoint or dedicate someone or something to a specialized purpose. At its most literal meaning, it means to pour or place oil on something. We see it, for instance, when large, seagoing vessels are *christened*. Here, we observe a christening of a very special kind: the Lord is being anointed . . . to die. The woman's act will become a living memorial. And this act reminds us of the central purpose of Jesus' earthly mission: to die.

Throughout the Old Testament, God uses humans to convey words of warning and offer his message of hope. Samuel was such an agent; so was Elijah, and Elisha after him. In the New Testament, we see such agents continuing the prophetic task. John the Baptizer is probably the most notable. But here we see a perhaps unexpected prophet: a woman otherwise nameless in Mark's Gospel, but whose deed will outlive her in the memory of the global church.

1. What might Jesus mean in verse 7 by, "you always have the poor with you"? Does this suggest that Jesus doesn't care about the needs of poor people? Why or why not?

2. What aspects of the woman's act demonstrate a connection with the prophets mentioned above, including John the Baptizer? Might she also be considered a prophet in some way? If so, how?

3. Notice that the woman is never mentioned by name, but Jesus says she will be remembered wherever the gospel is preached. Why didn't Mark mention her name? Of what significance is this to you as you read her account?

THREE

The Passover Lamb

Exodus 12:3–6 *Tell all the congregation of Israel that on the tenth day of this month they shall take every man a lamb according to their fathers' houses, a lamb for a household;* *⁴and if the household is too small for a lamb, then a man and his neighbor next to his house shall take according to the number of persons; according to what each can eat you shall make your count for the lamb.* *⁵Your lamb shall be without blemish, a male a year old; you shall take it from the sheep or from the goats;* *⁶and you shall keep it until the fourteenth day of this month, when the whole assembly of the congregation of Israel shall kill their lambs in the evening.*

Understanding the Word. In the opening chapter of John's Gospel, John the Baptizer is baptizing in the wilderness. Of course, and as you might suspect, such a character would arouse interest. Local religious officials went out to investigate him. John's responses to their questions may have caught them off guard, especially when John saw Jesus coming and declared, "Behold, the Lamb of God, who takes away the sin of the world!" (John 1:29).

So what does this have to do with Exodus, and what does Exodus have to do with Mark?

When Jesus directed his disciples to prepare for the celebration of Passover, he was following typical Jewish custom. That custom was an annual meal dedicated to the memory of God's liberation of the Hebrews from Egyptian slavery. The opening chapters of Exodus give us the story.

After nine very impressive plagues, Pharaoh's heart remained hard, and he refused to release the Hebrews from bondage. God therefore instructed Moses and his camp to prepare for the tenth and final plague: the death of the firstborn of every household in Egypt. However, the Hebrews would be spared if they followed directions. Their charge was to sacrifice a spotless lamb, share it as part of a communal meal, then swab some of the blood from the lamb on the outer edges of each doorpost as a sign to the angel of death sent by God to smite the firstborn. When the angel would see a doorpost appropriately swabbed, he would "pass over" the house, thus sparing those inside. The annual festival of Passover commemorates this act.

John identifies Jesus as the Passover Lamb. Further, Jesus knew going into his last meal with his disciples that they would need to understand—at some level—what was about to happen to him.

> And as they were eating, he took bread, and blessed, and broke it, and gave it to them, and said, "Take; this is my body." (Mark 14:22)

Sitting at table with his disciples, Jesus commemorated his last experience of the Jewish Passover. Moving forward, there would no longer be a need for a lamb, for Jesus as the Lamb of God was about to accomplish for humanity what no animal ever could. His sacrifice would be sufficient to take away the sins of the entire world. Thus, in the same evening, Jesus gave to his followers a new act of remembrance: the Eucharist. We know it in its original setting as the Last Supper, but we also know it in our worship today as Holy Communion.

Thus we see a thread of continuity beginning with God's saving of his people, Israel. That thread passes through Jesus' redefinition of the Passover meal amid the Last Supper, and comes to us today as Holy Communion. In it, we partake of the bread of the body that was broken in place of animals sacrificed by human hands.

1. In your view, how is Jesus the Passover Lamb, or—as John declared—"the Lamb of God"?

2. What is your typical experience with Holy Communion? What do you think happens when you partake of the bread and the wine? Based on your understanding of Holy Communion, what's the point of it?

3. How does the connection between the Passover meal of the Old Testament, the Last Supper of the New Testament, and the celebration of the Eucharist today shape your experience of Holy Communion?

FOUR

Ethics and Eschatology

Mark 14:23–25 *And he took a cup, and when he had given thanks he gave it to them, and they all drank of it.* ²⁴*And he said to them, "This is my blood of the covenant, which is poured out for many.* ²⁵*Truly, I say to you, I shall not drink again of the fruit of the vine until that day when I drink it new in the kingdom of God."*

Understanding the Word. Some of the questions I regularly get from my kids relate to heaven. Some time ago, our young sons were trying to wrap their minds around eternity. They were struggling with the concept of "forever." They also struggle with other ideas about heaven. They ask questions like, "What will my body be like? Who will be there? What will I do? What if I get bored?"

I remember wrestling with the concept of eternity. I still do. I also wrestle with some of these other questions as well. I must say, though, that my views of heaven are a bit different these days than they were in my earlier days.

A few years ago, I heard Randy Maddox speak on Wesley's view of salvation. Doctor Maddox is a very prominent Wesley scholar. He began his presentation by talking about how human views of heaven have evolved over the ages. Our modern notions of angels with wings, harps, and halos, floating around in diapers on puffy white clouds really have origins centuries ago. Those images have little to do with the biblical concept of eternity, and Wesley was committed to the idea that Scripture speaks of salvation *holistically*, meaning that God's plan for the redemption of his creation includes *all* of creation, including our bodies. The idea of bodiless spirits floating around in space is really a product of Greek thought dating at least as far back as Plato. The Bible counters that vision by telling us that we will continue to have bodily existence, but of a different kind. Jesus refers to that in our passage for today.

Jesus himself gives us some sense of the afterlife. Although his resurrected body bore the marks of crucifixion (see John 20:24–28), he was nevertheless bodily resurrected. Now this raises a whole bunch of questions that we have neither the time nor the space to investigate, but we can say this: if God intends to give the world an extreme makeover in the age to come, and if eternal life is available to us in that age, then it stands to reason that we will have bodies, senses, and capacities that are in some way like those we have today. Rather than imagine harps and halos, I think we need to rethink heaven. Here's what I say to my boys: "If God were to offer you life on earth forever, only without all the bad stuff, and you would never die, and you would never get bored, would you take that offer?"

Their answer is yes, and so is mine. The key is the part about boredom. Boredom (or lack of contentment) is a product of our fallen state. Restlessness is a result of Eve's and Adam's first sin in the garden, when having the entire garden except for one tree simply wasn't good enough. They passed that gene on to us. Part of the good news of the world to come is that there will be no room or need for boredom. Every day will be a delight.

If I meet my favorite comedian in heaven, I'll most certainly ask him to tell me a joke. When he does, I'll probably laugh until I can't breathe, because I think he's that funny. When I catch my breath, he'll look me straight in the eye and say, "Brad, come back tomorrow and I'll tell it to you again." And because a good joke is always a good joke in a world untainted by boredom, I'll come back the next day and laugh until I can't breathe all over again.

Although this portrait of heaven is probably faulty on a number of levels, I think it rings a bit truer to the biblical portrait of eternity than our harps and halos scenario. Further, I think it points to a view of salvation that actually begins in the here and now. When Jesus came to earth, he brought the kingdom of heaven with him. We pray, in fact, that God's will would be done on earth as it is in heaven (Matt. 6:10). With this view of the end in mind, one can see how our eschatology should inform our ethics, and this is the precise point Randy Maddox rightly makes about Wesley's view of salvation.

1. What is your earliest memory of the idea of heaven? How did you imagine it?

2. Prior to this study, what has been your most recent view of heaven? What's it like? How excited about it are you? How excited would others be hearing you describe your view of heaven?

3. What do you think about the definition offered above that suggests heaven will be much like this world, minus all of the evil in it? Is this a more compelling vision of heaven? Would it be more compelling to others as they might hear you describe it? Why or why not?

FIVE

Peter's Denial . . . and Recovery

Mark 14:29–30, 72 *Peter said to him, "Even though they all fall away, I will not." ³⁰And Jesus said to him, "Truly, I say to you, this very night, before the cock crows twice, you will deny me three times. . . ."*

⁷²And immediately the cock crowed a second time. And Peter remembered how Jesus had said to him, "Before the cock crows twice, you will deny me three times." And he broke down and wept.

Understanding the Word. A common tactic of many (if not most) New Testament scholars is to accentuate the failures of Jesus' disciples in Mark. The tactic is not unwarranted, as the disciples do indeed err time and time again. We see it when James and John request seats next to Jesus in the age to come (10:37). We see it when the disciples worry that they don't have anything to eat on the boat (8:16). We see it when Judas betrays Jesus (14:10). We see it when the disciples twice fall asleep while Jesus prays (14:37, 40). And we see it when the disciples abandon Jesus in his darkest hour.

But no one seems to bumble more than Peter. It was Peter whom Jesus rebuked, calling Peter "Satan" (8:33). It was Peter who didn't know what to say at the transfiguration of Jesus, blurting out, "Let me put up some tents for you guys!" (9:5–6). And it was Peter who denied even knowing Jesus . . . three times (14:66–72).

Criticism of Peter is justified. I suspect that Peter himself would be his own worst critic.

However, let's consider this: it was Peter who walked away from the only life he knew when Jesus called him out of the blue (1:18). It is Peter who is named first among any listing of the disciples. It was Peter who rightly declared Jesus to be the Christ (8:29). And it was Peter who delivered the bombshell Pentecost sermon in Acts 2 that led to the growth and rapid expansion of the church.

Clearly, Peter's performance deserves at least mixed reviews.

If we judge Peter and the other disciples by standards of perfection (that is, fully living into everything that Jesus asked of them), of course they fail. Who can possibly measure up to that? However, if we judge them by our own performance, the disciples emerge as rock stars, well-deserving of positions of prominence.

The good news for us is this: even if we falter, there's hope for recovery. In John's Gospel, Jesus asks Peter three times if Peter loves him (21:15–17). Commentators often suggest that this represents Jesus' intention of restoring Peter to right standing by giving him three opportunities to demonstrate his allegiance to Jesus, one for each time Peter denied Jesus. Whether or not this is the right interpretation, the fact remains that Jesus did not give up on Peter, despite Peter's worst failings. I think we need to cut Peter and the boys some slack. Maybe we need to also cut ourselves some slack.

1. In your reading of Mark up to this point, how would you rate the disciples' performance on a scale of one to ten? Are they heroes worth imitating, or dimwits to be pitied?

2. Think about the saints around you (i.e., faithful Christian believers). How does their faithfulness compare to that of the disciples as portrayed in Mark?

3. Think about your own witness to the world. How does your faithfulness compare to that of the disciples? How would others characterize your witness and faithfulness?

4. Who is a harsher critic of your walk with Jesus: you or those who know you?

COMMENTARY NOTES

General Comments. At this point, we must give a bit of attention to the notion of "time" in Mark's Gospel. On one hand, the movie reel definitely seems to be slowing down. On the other hand, the various timing cues that Mark gives us must be understood not as we reckon time today, but within an ancient Near Eastern understanding.

For example, the notion of "day" within Jewish circles was not the typical way we formulate it today. Our calendar days begin and end at midnight, or 12:00 a.m. Alternatively, we sometimes describe our days as occupying the period from wake up (typically sunrise) to bedtime (roughly sunset). Jews in the first century figured their time differently; they understood a "day" to begin at sunset, and end on the following sunset. And because the Jewish Sabbath was Saturday instead of Sunday, their weekly day of rest actually began on Friday evening. (For an interesting glimpse of how this was practiced even into much more recent times, watch *Fiddler on the Roof.*)

Another way of appreciating Mark's use of time is to know that the hours of the day were figured on the solar cycle. Sunrise was the "zero" hour, and the hours were marked principally by three-hour divisions. As you read the Gospels, you'll note that the majority of time demarcations are given in these increments: the third hour, the sixth hour, the ninth hour, etc. Although there are exceptions, this tends to be the general practice. Sunset would then constitute the twelfth hour, after which the night hours would be divided into three-hour periods, or "watches" (see Mark 6:48).

General Comments. Jewish life was largely ordered by a system that combined political and religious elements. As such, the Jews would not have observed a separation of church and state as we do today. The Jewish religious establishment consisted primarily of members who served on a central religious council, called the Sanhedrin. Like our Congress in the US, the Sanhedrin consisted of members of different parties (so to speak): the Pharisees and the Sadducees.

As we've discussed earlier, it is not completely accurate to characterize all members of a given party as strictly committed to the party line. For instance, all four Gospel writers mention Joseph of Arimathea as requesting Jesus' dead body from Pilate. Mark tells us that he was a respected member of the Jewish council and was himself seeking the kingdom of God (15:43). Luke reports that Joseph was "a good and righteous man" (Luke 23:50). John informs us that Joseph actually feared the Jews because of his relationship to Jesus (John 19:38).

Day 2. Although we can't be absolutely certain as to the significance of this act, it does seem rather apparent that this woman is symbolically preparing Jesus' body for burial. Compare the account in John 19:39, where we learn that "Nicode'mus also, who had at first come to him by night, came bringing a mixture of myrrh and aloes, about a hundred pounds' weight."

Day 3. The word *Eucharist* comes from a Greek word meaning "to give thanks" or "thanksgiving."

WEEK ELEVEN

GATHERING DISCUSSION OUTLINE

A. Open session in prayer. Ask for specific celebrations of God's goodness.

B. What new insights have you gained from this week's reading? What has encouraged you? What has challenged you?

C. View video for this week's readings.

D. Discuss questions selected from daily readings.

   1. **KEY OBSERVATION:** The way Mark tells his story highlights the themes of and contrast between *communion* and *betrayal.*

      DISCUSSION QUESTION: Why might Mark have structured this part of his message this way? What might he be suggesting about the human condition? How might this possibly address our own walks with Christ?

   2. **KEY OBSERVATION:** The woman's anointing of Jesus brought to reality the purpose of Jesus as *the anointed Son.*

      DISCUSSION QUESTION: In Week 7, I mentioned Dietrich Bonhoeffer, who famously said, "When Christ calls a man, he bids him come and die." How did Jesus demonstrate this principle himself? How does or should this affect a believer's understanding of Christian discipleship, and what would or could it mean to "come and die"?

   3. **KEY OBSERVATION:** As God's anointed, Jesus became the new Passover Lamb.

DISCUSSION QUESTION: What are your views of Holy Communion? What happens in that special moment in your life when you partake of the body and blood of Jesus? How does he serve as the Lamb of God for you?

4. **KEY OBSERVATION:** Eschatology (our view of the end) should inform our ethics (our conduct and the way we decide between good and bad moral choices).

   DISCUSSION QUESTION: Why is it important to have a biblical (rather than a popular) view of eternity? What are the consequences of maintaining a false or inadequate view of heaven? If we have a compelling vision of eternity, how will that impact the way we live life today?

5. **KEY OBSERVATION:** As followers of Jesus, we will certainly have some wins and some losses with regard to the practice of our discipleship.

   DISCUSSION QUESTION: Does knowing that Jesus forgave Peter and restored him to right relationship excuse us from our responsibility to be faithful disciples? If so, what responsibility, if any, do we have as followers of Jesus to exercise ethical conduct? If not, how do we avoid being overly burdened with guilt and shame?

E. What facts and information presented in the commentary portion of the lesson help you understand the weekly Scripture?

F. Close session with prayer. Ask for specific concerns to be brought before our Lord.

WEEK TWELVE

Mark 15:1–16:8

Black Friday

INTRODUCTION

I vividly remember my trip back home from Florida, where I had attended the funeral for the father of one of my very dearest friends. At the various airport terminals, it seemed that everyone was talking about Mel Gibson's recent release, *The Passion of the Christ*. Because I was traveling alone and had not yet seen the movie (it had just opened in theaters), I was not a part of any of those conversations, but I heard lots of them. It was profoundly impactful.

When I finally made it to the theater to see it, I was with my wife. We had just had our first son, and we were out for a rare date during those early months of parenthood. We entered the theater braced for the impact. Not only had we heard from numerous of our friends about the graphic nature of the film, but we knew all too well how the story ends: Jesus dies, but he rises again.

Knowing the story didn't really soften the impact of the film. I'm sure my wife felt as I did when we anxiously waited for the first harm to be inflicted upon Jesus. As the movie progressed, I began to sense a growing eagerness for Jesus to die. Yes, I wanted him to die, and for no other reason than to end his suffering. But his end didn't come quickly . . . the suffering went on, and on, and on.

When he finally breathed his last, I felt enormous relief. Not joy, not exhilaration, but the kind of peace that comes with admitting defeat. Of course, I rejoiced inwardly when the scene shifts and the view we have is from within the tomb as the stone rolls away, letting in a cascading flood of light. However, the actors in the real-life drama did not exactly know how this story was going to end. For us as movie-goers, the space of time between Jesus' death and his resurrection on Easter morning was very, very small. A few seconds to a few minutes at most. For them, it was thirty-six agonizing hours.

And for Jesus, the last hours of his life were filled with shame and humiliation . . . on a scale of epic proportions.

ONE

Jesus before Pilate

Mark 15:1–5 *And as soon as it was morning the chief priests, with the elders and scribes, and the whole council held a consultation; and they bound Jesus and led him away and delivered him to Pilate. ²And Pilate asked him, "Are you the King of the Jews?" And he answered him, "You have said so." ³And the chief priests accused him of many things. ⁴And Pilate again asked him, "Have you no answer to make? See how many charges they bring against you." ⁵But Jesus made no further answer, so that Pilate wondered.*

Understanding the Word. Friday, 6:00 a.m. IST (Israel Standard Time)— After a middle-of-the-night clandestine meeting of the Jewish council, Jesus is taken before the Roman governor, Pontius Pilate. Sleep escaped Jesus, and he must have been in a bit of a daze.

Pilate began what would have been an otherwise ordinary day for him. As an administrative official over the Judean province, he had the authority to grant or deny judicial requests recommended by the Jews subjected to Rome. We can't know what time Pilate rose to begin his day, but it was likely early; officials at that level tend to have very long, full days. The Jewish authorities interrupted Pilate's schedule to bring a request regarding one whom they considered a traitor to Jews and Rome. Pilate accepted the appointment.

The governor apparently knew a bit about Jesus. And what a curiosity Jesus must have seemed. Weary from lack of sleep, having been smacked around by the Sanhedrin, and—most curious of all—silent before his accusers, Jesus must have been something of an enigma to Pilate; certainly not what he expected from the so-called King of the Jews.

One of the things that we need to observe here is Jesus' silence. As we'll see in tomorrow's lesson: "He was oppressed, and he was afflicted, yet he opened not his mouth; like a lamb that is led to the slaughter, and like a sheep that before its shearers is dumb, so he opened not his mouth" (Isa. 53:7).

Central to Jesus' identity and function as the anointed One is his refusal to make claims about himself. Recall from an earlier lesson that an important aspect of Jewish thought was the performance of miracles as a way of authenticating one's words. In rhetorical terms, such a demonstration is called an *inartificial proof*. What does this mean? Well, let's take its counterpart: the *artificial proof*. Here, "artificial" does not mean fake or false, but rather constructed. For example, an "artifice" is a building or human-made structure. "Artificial" in this sense means humanly constructed. The Greeks (and, by extension, the Romans) built their cases on artificial, or human-devised arguments and proofs.

By contrast, the Jews relied on *inartificial* proofs: that is, proofs that are not of human origin or design. These include, as we saw early in this study, proofs by miracle, eyewitness testimony, and Scripture. Up to this point, all of these proofs have been adequately conveyed so as to determine without question that Jesus is exactly who he presents himself to be.

Before Pilate, Jesus only slightly breaks his pattern by affirming what Pilate seems to suggest: that Jesus is the King of the Jews. This is an important move on Jesus' part, because he surely recognizes that appeals to Scripture, eyewitnesses, and perhaps even miracles would be less than convincing. Pilate would need a direct claim, and Jesus gave that . . . but without violating his own commitments.

It's tempting to assign Pilate to one of two camps: the good guys or the bad guys. I think, as with life in general, Pilate is more complex than such a simple reduction. In fact, I think Pilate really didn't know what to do with Jesus, because Jesus didn't fit neatly and tidily into any preexisting categories Pilate held.

Jesus is like that.

1. Why would Jesus be seemingly hesitant to come right out and say, "Hey, everybody, I'm the Son of God!" Is he being coy, or is there deeper significance to his silence?

2. If someone appeared today claiming or having other people claim that he was the Son of God, what would convince you one way or the other? Why would this proof be decisive for you?

3. If you stood in the place of Pilate, what would you make of Jesus? How would you have handled the matter?

T W O

The Mocking of Jesus

Mark 15:25–32 *And it was the third hour, when they crucified him. ²⁶And the inscription of the charge against him read, "The King of the Jews." ²⁷And with him they crucified two robbers, one on his right and one on his left. ²⁹And those who passed by derided him, wagging their heads, and saying, "Aha! You who would destroy the temple and build it in three days, ³⁰save yourself, and come down from the cross!" ³¹So also the chief priests mocked him to one another with the scribes, saying, "He saved others; he cannot save himself. ³²Let the Christ, the King of Israel, come down now from the cross, that we may see and believe." Those who were crucified with him also reviled him.*

Understanding the Word. Friday, 9:00 a.m. IST—The King of the Jews meets utter humiliation.

It really should come as no surprise to us that Jesus would find his end this way. Recalling the central role of Isaiah in Mark's Gospel, we read:

> He was despised and rejected by men; a man of sorrows, and acquainted with grief; and as one from whom men hide their faces he was despised, and we esteemed him not.
>
> Surely he has borne our griefs and carried our sorrows; yet we esteemed him stricken, smitten by God, and afflicted. But he was wounded for our transgressions, he was bruised for our iniquities; upon him was the chastisement that made us whole, and with his stripes we are healed. All we like sheep have gone astray; we have turned every one to his own way; and the LORD has laid on him the iniquity of us all.
>
> He was oppressed, and he was afflicted, yet he opened not his mouth; like a lamb that is led to the slaughter, and like a sheep that before its shearers is dumb, so he opened not his mouth. By oppression and judgment he was taken away; and as for his generation, who considered that he was cut off

out of the land of the living, stricken for the transgression of my people? And they made his grave with the wicked and with a rich man in his death, although he had done no violence, and there was no deceit in his mouth. (Isa. 53:3–9)

From the beginning, the anointed one was destined to suffer at the hands of people. Mel Gibson's *The Passion of the Christ* has certainly brought us into touch with the brutal physical realities of crucifixion, but not enough attention has been given perhaps to Jesus' emotional suffering.

At a number of levels, Jesus' emotional and mental anguish had to be on par with his physical suffering. Consider the relationships he cultivated among the Twelve: one would betray him, two would ask for special standing in the coming age, one would deny him three times, and the rest would abandon him in his darkest hour.

Consider the religious authorities who represent the establishment Jesus had grown up with. Those persons entrusted with administering the Father's affairs on earth are the ones who nail him to a cross. Likewise, the political authorities tasked to maintain peace and civil rest are equally involved in his condemnation.

Although there are a few women who remain at his side until the end, they are strangely silent.

The most exalted human being ever to grace the surface of the planet dies amid the jeers, taunts, and ridicule of ignorant souls.

1. Perhaps you are all too familiar with the horror of Christ's physical suffering during his Passion. What thought have you given to his emotional suffering?

2. As you think about Jesus' life as recorded in Mark's Gospel up to this point, what aspect of his Passion do you think would be most painful to him emotionally?

3. In a related way, what aspect of Jesus' suffering is most difficult for you emotionally? What feelings do you experience as you read and reread the account of his crucifixion?

THREE

The Death of Jesus

Mark 15:33–37 *And when the sixth hour had come, there was darkness over the whole land until the ninth hour.* [34]*And at the ninth hour Jesus cried with a loud voice, "E'lo-i, E'lo-i, la'ma sabach-tha'ni?" which means, "My God, my God, why hast thou forsaken me?"* [35]*And some of the bystanders hearing it said, "Behold, he is calling Eli'jah."* [36]*And one ran and, filling a sponge full of vinegar, put it on a reed and gave it to him to drink, saying, "Wait, let us see whether Eli'jah will come to take him down."* [37]*And Jesus uttered a loud cry, and breathed his last.*

Understanding the Word. Friday, 12:00 p.m. IST—The death of the Christ is immanent. He has been awake since Thursday morning. He has been betrayed, beaten, mocked, abandoned, stripped, flogged, and nailed to a wooden crossbeam. Each breath is an agonizing effort in which he pushes upward against the spike in his feet so as to relieve the pressure on his chest cavity created by his suspended arms. In agony, he hangs there . . . minute after minute, hour after hour. The hope of humanity is dying on a tree. Even nature appears to grieve as a veil of darkness besets the scene.

I was recently asked what books—other than the Bible—have most influenced my Christian walk. I was surprised at how difficult this was to answer, not because there were so many, but because there were so few.

The Bible stands out in unparalleled ways, so removing it from the range of options makes the question harder. However, I do recall a book I read for a high school literature class. That book was Jim Bishop's *The Day Christ Died*. In it, Bishop walks the reader through the last, grueling day of Jesus' earthly life, hour by hour.

The book was arranged by chapters, each of which addressed an hour or so of Christ's life leading up to the crucifixion. As a physician, Bishop was able to walk the reader through the various physiological processes and sensations Jesus likely experience as he approached his death. It was a captivating but painful read. The only pauses in the hour-by-hour were two very large chapters located one-third and two-thirds of the way through the book. One chapter provided an overview of the Jewish world in which Jesus lived: its customs, rituals, and beliefs. The other chapter described the Roman world that created the backdrop to the story of Jesus. In it, Bishop explained Roman philosophy, military structure, and economic policies.

I remember wondering why the supplemental chapters on things like Roman and Jewish customs interrupted the flow of the account. Thirty years and three graduate degrees later, I now appreciate the importance of the context of the events. It is critical to understand that Jesus was Jewish, and never stopped being so. Likewise, the Roman Empire created the essential context for most, if not all, of what happens in the Gospels. But what really gripped me was the incredibly human perspective on the crucifixion of Jesus. It was painful, and glorious.

The details of Jesus' Passion are horrifying. And one can appreciate the humanity of Christ as he cries out in desperation to a God that seems to have abandoned him. Jesus the man has been pushed to the most extreme limits of the human experience. If anyone can relate to suffering, he can.

UPDATE
Friday, 3:00 p.m. IST—Jesus is dead.

1. In most communion liturgies, someone offers the bread and the wine (or juice) and says something like, "The body of Christ broken for you," and, "The blood of Christ shed for you." How does the physical brutality of Jesus' Passion impact your understanding of what it means for his body to be broken and his blood to be shed?

2. Does Jesus' physical suffering impact your view of your own sin? If so, how?

3. What sin remains in your life that is causing people (including yourself) to suffer emotionally or physically? In light of Jesus' sacrifice, what are you willing to do about that sin? (You may want to consider earnestly praying about your sin between now and the time you meet with your group. Your group might be an appropriate place for you to confess that sin.)

FOUR

"Truly This Was the Son of God"

Mark 15:38–39 *And the curtain of the temple was torn in two, from top to bottom. ³⁹And when the centurion, who stood facing him, saw that he thus breathed his last, he said, "Truly this man was the Son of God!"*

Understanding the Word. Our journey through Mark's Gospel comes to an end, or at least nearly so, with the death of Jesus. In reality, the entire narrative has been leading up to this moment, even as early as the first verse where we first came to know Jesus as the anointed Son of God. As we've further seen, his anointing was an anointing to suffer, to be crucified at the hands of angry men, and to die.

Throughout the narrative and at numerous key moments we gain glimpses into the nature of the Christ. One of the distinctives about Mark is his employment of questions raised about the identity and ministry of Jesus. These questions are typically structured in this way:

When Jesus exorcises a demon, the crowds marvel, saying, "What is this? A new teaching! With authority he commands even the unclean spirits, and they obey him." (Mark 1:27)

When scribes observe Jesus forgive the sins of a paralytic, they exclaim, "Why does this man speak thus? It is blasphemy! Who can forgive sins but God alone?" (Mark 2:7)

When scribes also observe Jesus dining with undesirables, they ask, "Why does he eat with tax collectors and sinners?" (Mark 2:16)

When Pharisees see Jesus' disciples gathering grain on the Sabbath, they complain, "Look, why are they doing what is not lawful on the sabbath?" (Mark 2:24)

When Jesus calms the storm, his disciples remark, "Who then is this, that even wind and sea obey him?" (Mark 4:41)

When Jesus preached to his hometown crowd, they wondered, "Where did this man get all this? What is the wisdom given to him? What mighty works are wrought by his hands!" (Mark 6:2)

When Jesus' disciples ate without ceremonially washing their hands, Pharisees challenged Jesus, saying, "Why do your disciples not live according to the tradition of the elders, but eat with hands defiled?" (Mark 7:5)

But if we stay close to the text of Mark, we notice that the questions continue:

Jesus to his disciples: "Who do men say that I am?" and then to Peter specifically, "But who do you say that I am?" (Mark 8:27–29)

The High Priest to Jesus: "Are you the Christ, the Son of the Blessed?" (Mark 14:61)

Pilate to Jesus: "Are you the King of the Jews?" (Mark 15:2)

People of all walks of life want to know about Jesus. And in an amazing irony, that identity is declared by the centurion at the foot of cross. Everything in Mark's Gospel leads up to the declaration made by a Gentile, a Roman soldier with blood on his hands, "Truly this man was the Son of God!" (Mark 15:39)

The opening verse of Mark continues to guide our reading. Not only is Jesus the *anointed*; he is also *the Son of God*. Taken with this opening assertion by Mark about Jesus in 1:1, the declaration of the centurion serves as a fitting bookend for a journey prescribed from the beginning. And that a Gentile would make the claim prefigures the church's mission to reach the entire world.

1. Suppose someone asked you at the beginning of this study, "Who is Jesus?" How would you have answered twelve weeks ago?

2. How has your understanding of Jesus changed over these past twelve weeks? If someone asked you today, "Who is Jesus?" would you respond any differently? If so, how?

3. Let's reframe the questions. If someone had asked you twelve weeks ago, "Who are you?" how would you have responded? Would you respond any differently today? If so, how?

FIVE

He Is Risen!

Mark 16:1–6 *And when the sabbath was past, Mary Mag'dalene, and Mary the mother of James, and Salo'me, bought spices, so that they might go and anoint him. ²And very early on the first day of the week they went to the tomb when the sun had risen. ³And they were saying to one another, "Who will roll away the stone for us from the door of the tomb?" ⁴And looking up, they saw that the stone was rolled back—it was very large. ⁵And entering the tomb, they saw a young man sitting on the right side, dressed in a white robe; and they were amazed. ⁶And he said to them, "Do not be amazed; you seek Jesus of Nazareth, who was crucified. He has risen, he is not here; see the place where they laid him."*

Understanding the Word. Friday, 6:00 p.m. IST—The sun sets. Jesus is dead. Women stand by with mouths agape. Joseph of Arimathea approaches Pilate, somberly asking permission to tend to Jesus' body. And darkness falls.

I *cannot imagine* (in fact, I don't want to imagine) what the next thirty-six hours were like for the followers of Jesus. Saturday had to simply be the WORST. DAY. EVER.

Mark continues to anchor his narrative to the concrete particularities of time during these closing scenes: "When the Sabbath was past . . . very early on the first day of the week . . . when the sun had risen." The women who stood by as Jesus breathed his last are now waiting for the dawn of a new day so that they can properly finish the burial process. In the last thirty-six hours, they could not even experience closure.

What happened next is simply unexplainable: the stone had been moved; the tomb was empty; Jesus was gone.

Sitting where Jesus should have been lying, an angelic messenger scares the women nearly to death. What he does next alters the landscape of reality. He utters the most profound words in human history: "Do not be amazed; you seek Jesus of Nazareth, who was crucified. He has risen, he is not here; see the place where they laid him" (Mark 16:6).

As a student and teacher of biblical Greek, I am sometimes struck by the original language of the New Testament. One of the most striking moments for me was when I read this for the first time: "*kai estaurōsan auton*" (Mark 15:25 GNT).

Literally, "and they crucified him." The starkness of this hit me like a punch in the gut. There it was. They really did it. What has struck me in an even larger way, though, is the impact of this: "*ēgerthē*" (Mark 16:6 GNT).

Literally, "he was raised."

Imagine what the world would be like had this fact not been recorded, much less had never happened. No single word in the annals of time has had more significance for the course of human affairs that this one: *ēgerthē*, "he was raised."

The claims of the Christian faith rise and fall on this utterance. Despite the fact that Mark's narrative comes to a complete stop as the women flee the tomb in fear, God awaits his curtain call. The story hasn't ended. No, it's just beginning. Jesus Christ has overcome death. The grave could not hold him.

Jesus Christ has risen. He has risen, indeed.

1. Take a moment and try to think through the time period from Friday night to Sunday morning and what the experience must have been like for the followers of Jesus. Has there ever been a moment in your life where you felt that hopeless? When was it?

2. Now think about the women's experience when they arrived to find the empty tomb. What do you suppose they were thinking? What would you have thought initially?

3. Jesus, the anointed Son of God, conquered the grave. Death could not hold him. He lives again, and he offers life to whoever believes in him. How will you respond to that fact tomorrow?

COMMENTARY NOTES

Day 5. Throughout this study we've had a chance to look at a number of issues related to the original Greek of Mark's Gospel. One of the distinctive features of the Greek of Mark's time is its efficiency: Koiné (or "common") Greek, though perhaps a bit wordier that classical Greek, nevertheless uses an economy of words when compared to the English language. An example is from a passage we read in our first week. In Mark 1:5, Mark reports that all of the Judean countryside and all of the Jerusalemites *were being baptized* by John. In the Greek, Mark needs to use only one word to say that "they were being baptized": *ebaptizonto*. In the space of one word, Mark is able to communicate what takes four words in English.

Day 5. Recall from the Commentary Notes in Week 1 that the oldest manuscripts of Mark's Gospel conclude with 16:8. It would seem that 16:9–20 was added at a later date.

WEEK TWELVE

GATHERING DISCUSSION OUTLINE

Special Note: If circumstances allow, arrange to share Holy Communion with your group this week. See Discussion Question 3 below for an appropriate time in the meeting to do so.

A. Open session in prayer. Ask for specific celebrations of God's goodness.

B. What new insights have you gained from this week's readings? What has encouraged you? What has challenged you?

C. View video for this week's readings.

D. Discuss questions selected from daily readings.

1. **KEY OBSERVATION:** Jesus defied human attempts to place him in a box.

DISCUSSION QUESTION: In what ways do our perceptions of Jesus fail to adequately capture his divine nature? What images or stereotypes cause false perceptions of him to endure? (Think especially of Jesus as portrayed in things like classical art, children's Bibles, contemporary Christian music, etc.)

2. **KEY OBSERVATION:** Jesus' emotional suffering may have been as intense (or even more so) than his physical suffering.

DISCUSSION QUESTION: What aspect of Christ's Passion pains you most? Why is this aspect particularly painful for you? Are there any experiences in your own life that cause you to more closely relate to Jesus' emotional anguish? If so, please share with the group (as much as you are willing).

3. **KEY OBSERVATION:** Jesus' body was broken and his blood was shed for the forgiveness of ours sins.

    DISCUSSION QUESTION: What does it mean to take and eat the bread, and to take and drink the cup? Before doing so, what sins would you like to confess to your group?

4. **KEY OBSERVATION:** Much of Mark's Gospel is centered on the identity of Jesus. At important points (namely, the beginning, midpoint, and end) Mark makes it clear that Jesus is the Son of God.

    DISCUSSION QUESTION: Who is Jesus to you? Consider taking turns around the table completing the sentence, "To me, Jesus is . . ."

5. **KEY OBSERVATION:** Jesus Christ is risen. He is risen, indeed.

    DISCUSSION QUESTION: Where will you go from here? If you have not surrendered your life to Jesus as an act of repentance, would you like to do so right now? If you already have surrendered your life to Jesus, would you like to renew that commitment now? As you consider choosing to follow Jesus or simply renewing your commitment to him, reach out to your group as a means of holding you accountable to cultivating a climate conducive for your own growth in Christ.

E. What facts and information presented in the commentary portion of the lesson help you understand the weekly Scripture?

F. Close session with prayer. Ask for specific concerns to be brought before our Lord.